TVSK ● IVORIES

The phrase "it's a classic" is much abused. Still there may be some appeal in the slant of the cap Overlook sets in publishing a list of books the editors at Overlook feel have continuing value, books usually dropped by other publishers because of "the realities of the marketplace." Overlook's Tusk Ivories aim to give these books a new life, recognizing that tastes, even in the area of so-called classics, are often time-bound and variable. The wheel comes around. Tusk Ivories begin with the hope that modest printings together with caring booksellers and reviewers will reestablish the books' presence and engender new interest.

As, almost certainly, American publishing has not been generous in offering readers books from the rest of the world, for the most part, Tusk Ivories will more than just a little represent fiction from European, Asian, and Latin American sources, but there will be of course some "lost" books from our own shores, too, books we think deserve new recognition and, with it, readers.

The Long Voyage

Jorge Semprun

Translated from the French by Richard Seaver

TV∫K ● IVORIES

Published by The Overlook Press

This edition first published in the United States in 2005 by
The Overlook Press, Peter Mayer Publishers, Inc.
Woodstock & New York

WOODSTOCK:
One Overlook Drive
Woodstock, NY 12498
www.overlookpress.com
[for individual orders, bulk and special sales, contact our Woodstock office]

NEW YORK:
141 Wooster Street
New York, NY 10012

Originally published in Paris, France by Libraire Gallimard
under the title *Le Grand Voygage* © 1963 by Editions Gallimard

Translation copyright © 1964 by Richard Seaver

Cataloging-in-Publication Data is available from the Library of Congress

Manufactured in Canada
ISBN 1-58567-639-X
1 3 5 7 9 8 6 4 2

for Jaime
because he is
sixteen years old

I

There is the cramming of the bodies into the boxcar, the throbbing pain in the right knee. The days, the nights. I force myself and try to count the days, to count the nights. Maybe that will help me see clearly. Four days, five nights. But I must have counted wrong, or else some of the days must have turned into nights. I have a surplus of nights, more nights than I can use. One morning, that much is sure, it was in the morning that this voyage began. All that day. Then a night. In the half-light of the boxcar I raised my thumb. My thumb for that first night. And then another day. We were still in France, and the train hardly moved. Now and then we heard voices, trainmen's voices, more distant than the sound of the sentinels' boots. Forget that day, it was a day of despair. Another night. I raise a second finger in the half-light. A third day. Another night. Three fingers of my left hand. And today. So, four days and three nights. We're advancing toward the fourth night, the fifth day. Toward the fifth night, the sixth day. But is it we who are advancing? We're motionless, stacked in on top of one another, it's the night that is advancing, the fourth night, advancing toward the motionless corpses we are destined to be. I burst out laughing: this is really going to be the Night of the Bulgarians.

"Save your strength," the guy says.

In the wild confusion of the ascent at Compiègne, amid the bellows and blows, he happened to be next to me. He looks as though that's how he's spent his whole life, traveling with a hundred and nineteen other guys in a padlocked boxcar. "The window," he said succinctly. With three steps and three jabs of his elbow, he cleared us a path to one of the openings covered with barbed wire. "Breathing's the main thing, see, being able to breathe."

"What good does it do to laugh?" the guy says. "You wear yourself out for nothing."

"I was thinking of the next night," I tell him.

"That's stupid as hell," the guy says. "Think of the nights already past."

"You're reason personified."

"Screw you," he replies.

This makes four days and three nights that we've been jammed against each other, intertwined, his elbow in my ribs, my elbow in his stomach. In order for him to be able to put both feet flat on the floor, I have to stand on one leg. That way we gain a few inches and take turns resting.

Around us, the semi-darkness, with labored breathing and sudden, terror-stricken outbursts when someone collapses. When they counted off a hundred and twenty of us in front of the boxcar, I felt a cold shiver run up and down my spine as I tried to picture what it might be like. It's even worse.

I close my eyes; I open my eyes again. It's not a dream.

"You see that?" I ask him.

"So?" he says. "We're out in the country."

Yes, the country. The train is inching along over high ground. There is snow, tall pines, calm wisps of smoke in the gray sky.

He glances out.

"It's the Moselle valley."

"How do you know?" I asked him.

He looks at me pensively and shrugs his shoulders.

"What other way is there to go?"

The guy's right, what other way is there to go God knows where? I close my eyes, and it hums softly inside me: the Moselle valley. I was lost in the semi-darkness, but now the universe is taking shape again around me on this waning winter afternoon. The Moselle valley does exist, it must be on the maps, in the atlases. In school, at the

Henri IV Lycée, we used to give the geography professor a rough time, my memory of the Moselle certainly can't come from there. I don't believe I learned a single geography lesson that whole year. Bouchez was furious with me. How is it possible for the head of the class in philosophy not to have any interest in geography? There was no connection, of course. But he was furious with me. Especially after that affair of the trains in Central Europe. I had played it up big and even supplied him with the names of the trains. I remember the Harmonika Zug, among others I'd given him the Harmonika Zug. "Good paper," he had noted, "but based too exclusively on personal reminiscences." Then, during class, when he had handed back the papers, I had pointed out to him that I had no personal recollection of Central Europe. Central Europe? Never been there myself. All I had done was cull some pertinent information from Barnabooth's travel diaries. You don't know A. O. Barnabooth, Monsieur Bouchez, the main character in one of Valéry Larbaud's books? To tell the truth, I still don't know whether he knew A. O. Barnabooth. He lost his temper, and I was almost sent before the discipline committee.

But now here is the Moselle valley. I close my eyes, savoring this darkness which unfolds within me, savoring this certainty of the Moselle valley, outside there beneath the snow. This dazzling certainty of the gray tints, the tall pines, the prim villages, the calm smoke in the winter sky. I force myself to keep my eyes closed as long as possible. The train is moving slowly, to the monotonous sound of the axle. Suddenly it whistles. It must have rent the winter landscape, as it rent my heart. I open my eyes, quickly, to take the countryside by surprise, to catch it unawares. There it is. It's simply there, it has nothing else to do. I could die right now, standing here in the boxcar crammed with future corpses, and it would still be there.

The Moselle valley would be there, beneath my lifeless gaze, sumptuously beautiful, like a Brueghel winter scene. We could all die, I and this guy from Semur-en-Auxois and the old man a while back who was screaming and wouldn't stop, his neighbors must have knocked him out, not a peep out of him now, it would still be there, beneath our lifeless gazes. I close my eyes, I open my eyes. My life is nothing more than this blinking of my eyes which reveals the Moselle valley to me. My life has left me, it hovers over this winter valley, it is this valley, soft and warm in the winter cold.

"What are you playing?" says the guy from the Semur. He watches me closely, trying to understand.

"Don't you feel well?" he asks.

"I'm all right," I tell him. "Why?"

"You're blinking your eyes like a sweet-young-thing," he declares. "A real show."

I let him talk, I don't want to be distracted.

The train swings around an embankment on the side of a hill. The valley unfolds. I mustn't let my mind be distracted from this quiet joy. The Moselle, its slopes, its vineyards beneath the snow, its winegrowers' villages beneath the snow, come in to me through my eyes. There are things, people or objects about which you say that you have them "coming out of your ears." That's an expression that has always amused me. They are the objects that encumber you, the people you can't bear, whom you reject, metaphorically, out of your ears. They return to their existence outside me. Rejected by me, made trivial, diminished by my act of rejection. My ears become the drain for excessive pride, the very symbols of a mind which deems itself sovereign. This woman, that friend, that music? Finished, drop the subject, out through the ears. But the Moselle is the exact opposite. The Moselle comes in to me through my eyes, inundates my gaze, gorges my soul, which is like a sponge, with slow waters. I am nothing but this Moselle which invades my being through the eyes. I have to concentrate on this savage pleasure.

"They make good wine in this region," says the guy from Semur.

He wants us to talk. Obviously he hasn't guessed that I'm in the throes of drowning in the Moselle, but he feels there's something suspicious about my silence. He thinks we ought to be serious, the guy from Semur does, this voyage to a camp in Germany is no laughing matter, nothing to blink your eyes about like a blithering idiot staring at the Moselle. He comes from a winegrowing region, so he clings to the Moselle vineyards, under a thin layer of powdery snow. Vineyards are a serious matter, he knows whereof he speaks.

"A good little white wine," the guy says. "Not as good as Chablis, though."

He's taking his revenge, that figures. The Moselle valley holds us in its embrace, it is the gate of exile, a one-way ride, perhaps, but their good little wine is not up to the Chablis. That's some consolation, in a way.

He'd like to discuss the Chablis, I won't discuss the Chablis with him, in any case not right now. He knows that we have some similar past experiences, that we may even have run into each other without actually having met. He was a member of the Semur underground when Julien and I went there to bring them arms, after what happened at the sawmill. He'd like to evoke the memories we have in common. They're serious memories, like the vineyards and working in the vineyards. Solid memories. Who knows, is he suddenly afraid to be alone? I don't think so. Not yet anyway. It's my solitude he's afraid of, yes, no question about it. He thought that I was suddenly breaking down under the impact of this landscape, reddish brown against a white background. He thought that this landscape had touched me at some sensitive spot, that I was breaking down, suddenly going soft. The guy from Semur is afraid to leave me alone. He's offering me the memory of the Chablis, he wants us to drink together the new wine of shared memories. The wait in the forest, with the S.S. staked out in ambush along the roads, after what happened at the sawmill. Nighttime sorties, in the Citroën sedan with the broken windows, the machine gun aimed out at the shadows. Manly memories, in other words.

But I'm not breaking down, pal. Don't take my silence amiss. In a little while we'll talk. It was beautiful, Semur was beautiful in September. We'll talk about Semur. In fact, there's a story I haven't told you yet. Julien was put out at losing the motorcycle. A powerful Gnôme et Rhône, practically brand new. It had been left behind in the sawmill that night when the S.S. arrived in force and you had to take off for the wooded hills above. It annoyed Julien to lose that motorcycle. So he went back for it. The Germans had set up an outpost above the sawmill, on the other side of the water. We went there in broad daylight, threading our way through the sheds and in among the piles of wood. The motorcycle was there all right, concealed beneath some canvas covers, its tank half full. We pushed it out to the road. Obviously when the motor kicked over the Germans were going to react. There was a completely open stretch of road, a sharp grade. From the top of their observation post, the Germans were going to have a field day taking potshots at us. But Julien wanted that motorcycle, he really wanted it. I'll tell you that story in a little while, you'll be happy to learn that the motorcycle wasn't lost. We drove it to the Taboo maquis, up on the heights of Larrey, between Laignes and Chatillon. But I won't tell you how Julien died, what's the point of telling you how Julien died? Anyway, I still don't know that Julien is dead. Julien's not dead, he's on his motorcycle, with me, we're in the autumn sun racing toward Laignes, and the patrols of the Feld are worried about this phantom motorcycle on the autumn roads, they fire blindly at the phantom noise of a motorcycle on the golden autumn roads. I won't tell you how Julien died, there would be too many deaths to tell about. You'll be dead yourself before this voyage is over. Before we return from this voyage.

Even if all of us in this boxcar were dead, stacked in dead standing up, a hundred and twenty in this boxcar, the Moselle valley would still be there before our dead eyes. I don't want to lose sight of this fundamental certainty. I open my eyes. Here's the valley, fashioned by the work of centuries, the terraced vineyards along the slopes, beneath a thin layer of hard snow, scored with brownish trails. My look is nothing without this landscape. Without this scenery I would be blind. My gaze doesn't discover this landscape, it is revealed by this landscape. It is the light of this landscape which creates my look. It is the history of this landscape, the long history of this landscape's creation, through the work of the Moselle winegrowers, which gives my gaze, my entire being, its true consistency, its depth. I close my eyes. All that remains is the monotonous sound of the wheels on the tracks. All that remains is this absent reality of the Moselle, absent from me but present unto itself, such as the Moselle winegrowers have made it. I open my eyes, I close my eyes, my life is nothing but a blinking of the eyes.

"Are you having visions?" says the guy from Semur.

"As a matter of fact," I say, "I'm not."

"That's what it looks like. You look as though you don't believe what you're seeing."

"I do, though, I really do."

"Or else that you're about to kick off."

He looks at me warily.

"Don't let it worry you."

"You going to be all right?" he wants to know.

"Of course I'm going to be all right, I'm fine, really."

Suddenly there are shouts in the car, screams.

A violent thrust of the whole inert mass of jammed-in bodies literally glues us to the side of the car. Our faces graze the barbed wire covering the opening. We look out at the Moselle valley.

"That land is well cared for," says the guy from Semur.

I look out at that well-cared-for land.

"Winegrowers are winegrowers."

He turns his head slightly toward me and laughs mockingly.

"Can I quote you on that?"

"I meant..."

"Of course," he says impatiently, "you meant, it's obvious what you meant."

"You were saying that their wine can't compare with Chablis?"

He glances at me out of the corner of his eye. He must be thinking that my question's a trap. The guy from Semur finds me damn complicated. But it's not a trap. It's a question to renew the thread of our four days and three nights of conversation. I still don't know the Moselle wine. It was only later, in Eisenach, that I tasted it. On my way back from this journey. At a hotel in Eisenach where they had set up the repatriation center. A strange evening, that first evening of repatriation. Enough to make you sick. The fact is we were like fish out of water. That readaptation period was necessary, no question about it, to reacquaint us with the ways of the world. A hotel in Eisenach, with some American officers of the Third Army, some French and English officers from the military missions sent to the camp. The German personnel, all of them old, disguised as headwaiters and waiters. And girls. Lots of German, French, Austrian and Polish girls, and God knows what else besides.

A very proper evening, actually, very ordinary, everyone playing his role and doing his job. The American officers chewing their chewing gum and talking among themselves, drinking straight out of the bottles of their own whiskey. The English officers all alone, seemingly ill at ease at being on the Continent, in the midst of all that promiscuity. The French officers, surrounded by girls, managing very nicely to make themselves understood by all these girls of various origins. Everyone doing his job. The German headwaiters doing their job as German headwaiters. The girls from various countries doing their jobs as girls from various countries. And we doing our job as survivors of the death camps. A little like fish out of water, admittedly, but quite dignified, our skulls shaved, our striped burlap trousers shoved down into the boots we had retrieved from the S.S. warehouses. Out of place, but impeccably correct, telling our stories to these French officers who were pawing at the girls. Our ridiculous recollections of crematoriums and interminable roll calls in the snow. Then we sat down around a table to have dinner. There was a white tablecloth on the table, there were fish dishes, meat dishes, dessert dishes. Glasses of different shapes and colors, for the white wine, the red wine, for water. We laughed stupidly in the presence of these unaccustomed things. And we drank Moselle wine. This wine from the Moselle couldn't compare with Chablis, but it was Moselle wine.

I repeat my question, which isn't a trap. I still haven't drunk any Moselle wine.

"How do you know the wine from around here can't compare with Chablis?"

He shrugs his shoulders. It's so obvious. It so obviously can't compare with Chablis.

He's beginning to get on my nerves.

"In fact, how do you know this is the Moselle valley?"

He shrugs his shoulders, again it's so obvious.

"Listen, pal, don't be such a bloody bore. The railroad has to follow the valleys. What other way is there to go?"

"All right," I say, trying to be conciliatory. "But why the Moselle?"

"I tell you that's the way."

"But no one knows where we're going."

"Of course we know. How did you spend your goddamn time at Compiègne? We know we're going to Weimar."

At Compiègne I spent my goddamn time sleeping. At Compiègne I was alone, I didn't know a soul, and besides the departure of the convoy was announced for two days later. I spent my goddamn time sleeping. In Auxerre there were buddies I'd known for several months, prison had become bearable. But in Compiègne there were thousands of us, it was a real mess, I didn't know a soul.

"I spent my goddamn time sleeping. I was only at Compiegne a day and a half."

"And you were sleepy?" he says.

"It wasn't so much that I was sleepy," I answer. "I just didn't have anything else to do."

"And you managed to sleep with all the noise and confusion going on at Compiègne during those days?"

"I managed."

Then he explains to me that he was at Compiègne for several weeks. Time enough to learn a few things. It was the period of the mass departures for the camps. Summary information succeeded in filtering down. The camps in Poland were the worst, the German guards apparently talked about them in hushed tones. There was another camp, in Austria, that you had better avoid as well. Then there were lots of camps in Germany itself which were more or less the same. The eve of our departure we had learned that our convoy was headed toward one of these camps, near Weimar. And, quite simply, the way there was through the Moselle valley.

"Weimar," I say, "is a city in the provinces."

"All cities are in the provinces," he says, "except capitals."

We both laugh, since common sense is the most evenly divided thing in the world.

"I meant a provincial city."

"That's right," he says, "something like Semur, that's what you're implying."

"Maybe bigger than Semur, how should I know, certainly much bigger than Semur."

"But there's no camp in Semur," he says to me with a trace of hostility.

"Why not?"

"What do you mean, why not? Because. Are you insinuating there might be a camp in Semur?"

"And why not? It's a question of circumstance."

"The hell with circumstance."

"There are camps in France," I explain, "there might have been one in Semur."

"There are camps in France?"

He looks at me, taken aback.

"Of course."

"French camps, in France?"

"Of course," I repeat, "not Japanese camps. French camps, in France."

"It's true there's Compiègne. But I don't call that a French camp."

"There's Compiègne, which was a French camp in France before it became a German camp in France. But there are others which have never been anything but French camps in France."

I mention Argelès, Saint-Cyprien, Gurs, Chateaubriant.

"No shit," he mutters.

This revelation upsets him. But he quickly recovers.

"Have to explain that to me, pal," he says.

He doesn't question my statement concerning the existence of French camps in France. But still he refuses to be overwhelmed by the discovery. Have to fill him in. He doesn't question my statement, but it doesn't fit in with his idea of things. His is a strictly elementary notion, with all the good on one side and all the evil on the other. Most practical. It was no problem for him to explain it to me in a few sentences. He's the son of fairly well-to-do peasants, he would have liked to leave the country, become a mechanic, who knows, a metal fitter, a lathe operator, a driller, anything, beautiful work on beautiful machines, as he put it. And then there were the forced labor batallions, the S.T.O. It was obvious he wasn't going to let himself be carted off to Germany. Germany was a long way off, and besides, it's not France, and anyway, you don't go and work for the people who are occupying your country. So he had turned into a rebel, he had joined the underground. The rest followed from it quite simply, as a logical sequence. "I'm a patriot, y'know," he said to me. This guy from Semur really intrigued me, it was the first time I had ever seen a real flesh-and-blood patriot. Because he wasn't a nationalist, not one bit, he was a patriot. I had known a fair number of nationalists. The architect was a nationalist. He had blue eyes, a direct, open look staring steadily at the blue line of the Vosges. He was a nationalist, but he worked for Buckmaster and the War Office. Whereas the guy from Semur was a patriot, he couldn't have been less of a nationalist. He was my first flesh-and-blood patriot.

"All right," I tell him, "I'll explain it to you a little later."
"Why later?"
"I'm looking at the landscape," I answer, "let me look at the landscape."
"It's just country," he said with an air of disgust.
But he let me look at the country.
The train whistles. I suppose that a locomotive always has some logical reason for blowing its whistle. It has

some concrete meaning. But at night, in the hotel rooms we've rented near the railroad station, using false names, when we have trouble falling asleep because of the thoughts crowding into our minds, or that run rampant by themselves, in unfamiliar hotel rooms train whistles have an unexpected resonance. They lose their concrete, rational significance, they become a call, or an incomprehensible warning. The trains whistle in the night and you turn over in your bed, vaguely worried. That's certainly an impression that derives from cheap literature, but it's real all the same. My train whistles in the Moselle valley, and I watch the winter land-scape slipping by. Night is falling. There are some people out walking along the road that runs beside the track. They are going toward this little village crowned with quiet wreaths of smoke. Maybe they cast a glance in the direction of this train, an absent-minded glance, it's only a freight train like so many others that pass through. They are on their way home, what does this train mean to them, they have their own lives, their worries, their own problems. Seeing them walking down that road, as if it were the most simple thing in the world, I suddenly realize that I'm inside and they're outside. I'm overwhelmed by a profound, physical feeling of sadness. I'm inside, for months I've been inside, and the others are outside. It's not only the fact that they are free, which is also open to question. It's merely that they are outside, that for them there are roads, hedges beside the paths, fruit on the fruit trees, grapes on the vines. They, quite simply, are outside, and I am inside. It's not so much that I can't go where I want, we're never all that free to go where we want. I've never been really all that free to go where I wanted. I've been free to go where I had to go, and I had to get on this train, since I had to do the things which led me to this train. I was free, completely free, to get on this train, and I put that freedom to good use. I'm here, on this train. I'm here of my own free will, since I could have not been here. So it's not that at all. It's merely a physical feeling: we are inside. There's the outside and the inside, and I'm inside. It's a feeling of sadness, a physical feeling that courses through you, nothing more.

Later, that feeling became even more violent. At times, it became unbearable. Now I look at these people out walking and I don't yet know that this feeling of being inside is going to become unbearable. Perhaps I ought to talk only of these people out walking and of this feeling the way it was then, in the Moselle valley, so as not to upset the order of the story. But I'm the one writing this story, I'll do as I like. I could have refrained from mentioning the guy from Semur. He was with me on this voyage, he died from it, that's a story which, actually, is nobody's concern. But I chose to talk about it. First of all because of Semur-en-Auxois, because of the coincidence of traveling with a guy from Semur. I really like Semur, a place to which I've never since returned. I really liked Semur in the autumn. Julien and I went there with three suitcases full of plastic bombs and Sten guns. The railway workers helped us hide them until we made contact with the maquis. Then we carried them to the cemetery, that's where the boys went to pick them up. Semur was beautiful in the autumn. We stayed there with the boys for two days, up on the hill. The weather was fine, it was September as far as the eye could see. I decided to talk about the guy from Semur because of Semur, because of this voyage. He died right next to me, at the end of this voyage, I finished this voyage with his body standing beside me. I made up my mind to talk about him, it's nobody's concern, nobody's but mine. It's between the guy from Semur and me.

Anyway, when I describe this feeling of being inside which overwhelmed me in the Moselle valley, seeing these people walking down the road, I am no longer in the Moselle valley. Sixteen years have passed. I can't confine myself now to that particular moment. Other moments have superimposed themselves on that one, forming a whole with that violent feeling of physical sadness which filled me in the Moselle valley.

Generally it used to happen on Sunday. As soon as noon roll call was over, we had several hours to kill. The camp loudspeakers piped in sweet music to all the rooms. And it was in the spring that that feeling of being inside tended to become unbearable.

I went beyond the quarantine camp, into the small wood next to the "Revier." I used to stop at the edge of the grove. Beyond this point there was nothing but a bare strip of earth in front of the watchtowers and the electrified barbed wire. You could see the rich, loamy Thuringian plain. You could see the village on the plain. You could see the road that skirted the camp for a hundred yards. You could see the people out walking along the road. It was spring, it was Sunday, people were out walking. Sometimes there were children. They ran on ahead, shouting. There were women too, who stopped on the side of the road to pick the spring flowers. I was there, standing on the edge of the little wood, fascinated by these images of life outside. Yes, that was it, there was an inside and an outside. I used to wait there, in the breath of spring, for the strollers to return. They were on their way home, the kids were worn out, they were walking meekly beside their parents. The strollers were going home. Then I was all alone. Only the inside was left, and I was inside.

Later, a year later, it was spring again, it was April, I too walked along that road and went to that village. I was outside, but somehow I couldn't bring myself to enjoy being outside. It was all over, we were going to take this same voyage back in the opposite direction, but maybe you never take this voyage back in the opposite direction, maybe you can never erase this voyage. I don't know, really. For sixteen years I've tried to forget this voyage, and I did forget this voyage. No one around me thinks any more about my having made this voyage. But the fact is that I forgot this voyage while realizing full well that I would one day have to take it again. In five years, ten years, fifteen years, I would have to take this voyage all over again. It was all there, waiting for me: the Moselle valley, the guy from Semur, the village on the Thuringian plain, and the fountain in the village square to which I shall return to take a long drink of cold water.

Perhaps one can't take this voyage back in the opposite direction.

"Now what are you looking at?" says the guy from Semur. "You can't see anything any more."

He's right, it's dark outside.

"I wasn't looking any longer," I admit.

"That's a bad sign," he says tartly.

"Bad in what way?"

"In every way," he explains. "Looking without seeing, dreaming with your eyes open. That's a bad sign."

"And remembering?"

"Yes, remembering too. It's distracting."

"Distracting from what?" I ask him.

The guy from Semur never ceases to amaze me.

"It distracts you from the trip, it makes you soft. We have to hold out."

"Hold out for what? So we can tell about this voyage?"

"Of course not, so we can come back from it," he says sternly. "It would be too stupid, don't you think?"

"There are always a few who come back to tell the others."

"Count me in," he says. "But not to tell about it, that I don't give a damn about. Just to come back."

"Don't you think we ought to tell about it?"

"But there's nothing to tell. A hundred and twenty guys in a boxcar. Days and nights of traveling. Old men who go off their nuts and begin screaming. I'd like to know what there is to tell."

"And at the end of the line?" I ask him.

His breath comes in fits and starts.

"The end of the line?"

It's obvious he doesn't want to think about it. He's concentrating on the problems of the voyage. He doesn't want to think about what might be at the end of the line.

"One thing at a time," he says finally. "Don't you agree?"

"Of course I do. You're right. It was just an idle question."

"You're always asking idle questions," he says.

"That's my job," I reply.

He doesn't pursue it further. He must be wondering what kind of job it can be that obliges someone to keep asking idle questions.

"You're both dumb asses," says a voice behind us. "God-damn asses."

We don't answer, we've been all through this before.

"You stand there like dumb bastards, spieling on about your lives. Bastards, fucking bastards."

"I hear voices," says the guy from Semur.

"Voices from beyond the grave," I add.

We both laugh.

"Go ahead and laugh, you idiots, you can drown in your words. But your number's up. Tell about this trip? Pardon me for laughing, you dumb bastards. You're going to die like rats."

"In that case our voices are voices from beyond the grave too," says the guy from Semur.

We laugh even louder.

His voice is choked with rage, his insults are becoming methodical.

"When I think," the voice starts in again, "that it's because of guys like you that I'm here. Real bastards. They play at soldierboys and we're the ones who have to pay for it. Fucking bastards!"

It's been like that almost since the start of the voyage. From what we could gather, this character had a farm in a region where the underground was operating. He was taken in a general roundup, when the Germans decided to clean out the area.

"At night they race up and down the roads," says the voice filled with hate, "they blow up the trains, foul everything up, and then we pay for it."

"This character's beginning to get on my nerves," says the guy from Semur.

"Accuse me of having furnished those bastards with food! I'd rather have cut off my right hand, turn them in, that's what I should've done."

"That's enough," says the guy from Semur. "Just be careful you don't have something else cut off, like your balls, cut off in neat round slices, how about that?"

The voice screams with rage, terror, incomprehension.

"Shut up," says the guy from Semur, "shut up or I'll lay one on you."

The voice stops.

Early in the voyage, the guy from Semur had already laid a good one on him. The guy knows what to expect. It was a few hours after the departure. We had barely begun to realize that it wasn't some poor joke, that we really would have to remain cooped up like this for days and nights on end, jammed in, unable to breathe. The old men had already begun to panic, and to express it. They would never be able to hold out, they were going to die. They were right in fact, some of them were going to die. And then there were some voices that called for silence. One young guy—we gathered he belonged to some underground unit—said that he and his colleagues had managed to smuggle in some tools. As soon as it was dark, they were going to saw through the floorboards of the car. Those who wanted to try and escape with them had only to edge their way over to the hole and, when the train slowed down, drop through.

The guy from Semur glanced at me, and I nodded. We were for it, of course we were for it.

"You have to hand it to them," the guy from Semur murmured. "Sneaking those tools through all the searches, you really have to hand it to them."

In the ensuing silence, the guy from Semur spoke up.

"All right, friend, go to it. When you're ready, let us know so we can come over."

But that sentence evoked a chorus of protests. The discussion was endless. Everybody joined in. The Germans would discover the attempted escape and take reprisals. And besides, even if the escape were to succeed, not everyone would be able to get away; those left behind would be shot. There were quavering voices that begged, for the love of God, not to try anything so crazy. There were tremulous voices that spoke to us of their children, their beautiful children who would be left orphans. But we stilled those voices. It was during this discussion that the guy from Semur socked the other guy. That character didn't bother beating around the bush. He came right out and said that if we began to saw through the floor of the car, he would call the German sentinels the next time the train stopped. We looked at the guy, who was right behind us. Yes, he looked the part, no question about it. It was then that the guy from Semur laid one on him. There was an eddying swirl of bodies, a swaying movement. The man collapsed, his face covered with blood. When he got back to his feet, he saw himself surrounded by half a dozen hostile faces.

"Got the point?" a man with already graying hair said

to him, "got the point, you bastard? One suspicious move, just one, and I swear I'll strangle you."

The guy got the point. He got the point that he'd never have time to call a German sentinel, that he'd be dead first. He wiped the blood from his face, and his face was the mirror of hate.

"Shut up," the guy from Semur says to him now, "shut up or I'll lay one on you."

Since that discussion three days have passed, three days and three nights. The escape failed to materialize. During the first night, some guys in another car beat us to it. The train ground to a halt. We heard bursts of machine-gun fire, and searchlights swept the countryside. Then the S.S. came to make a car by car search. They clubbed us as we got down, they searched the guys one by one and made us remove our shoes. We had to ditch the tools before they reached our car.

"Say," the guy from Semur whispers.

It was the first time I had heard his voice that way, low and hoarse.

"What is it?" I ask.

"We ought to try and stay together. Don't you think so?"

"We are together."

"I mean afterward, when we get there. We ought to stay together when we get there."

"We'll try."

"It'll be easier for two, don't you think? It'll make it easier to hold out," says the guy from Semur.

"There ought to be more than just a couple of us together. Only two isn't going to be easy."

"Maybe," says the guy from Semur, "but that's already something."

Now night is falling, the fourth night, awakening the phantoms. In the black crush of the boxcar the men again find themselves alone, with their thirst, their fatigue, their anxiety. A heavy silence settles down, punctuated by a few indistinct but continuous moans. It's the same every night. Later, there will be the terrified screams of those who think they are dying. Nightmarish screams, that have to be silenced by any and all means. You shake the man screaming, his face convulsed, his mouth open. If you have to, you slap him. But now it's still the uneasy hour of memories. They rise to the throat, they choke you, they weaken the will. I expel memory. I'm twenty, I don't give a damn about memory. There's also another way. Put this voyage to good use by sorting things out. Draw up the balance sheet of the things in life that are really worth their weight and those that are not. The train whistles in the Moselle valley, and I let my light memories take wing. I'm twenty, I can still allow myself the luxury of choosing in life the things I'm going to assume and those I reject. I'm twenty, I can erase all kinds of things from my life. Fifteen years from now, when I write about this voyage, it will be impossible. Or at least I suspect it will. Not only will things weigh something in your life, they'll have a weight of their own. Fifteen years from now, memories won't be so light. The weight of your life may be something irreparable. But that night, in the Moselle valley, with the train whistling and my pal from Semur, I'm twenty years old and I don't give a damn about the past.

What carries the most weight in your life are the people you've known. This I realized that night, once and for all. I let the light things take wing, the pleasant memories which were of interest only to me. A tract of pines in Guadarrama. A ray of sunlight on the rue d'Ulm. Light things, full of an evanescent but absolute happiness. Yes, I said absolute. But what carries the most weight in your life are certain people you've known. Books and music are different. However enriching they may be, they are never anything but a way to reach people. This, of course, when they are real people. The others, in the final analysis, are a drag. That night I finally clarified that question. The guy from Semur sank into a sleep filled with dreams. He murmured some things I have no intention of repeating. It's easy to sleep standing up when you are caught in the gasping welter of bodies crammed into the boxcar. The guy from Semur was asleep standing up, in a sea of anguished murmurs. I simply felt that his body had grown heavier than before.

In my room in the rue Blainville, the three of us used to get together for hours on end, also in order to sort out everything imaginable. The room in the rue Blainville will weigh on my life, I could already tell, but that night in the Moselle valley I entered it permanently on the credit side of the balance sheet. We took a long detour to arrive at real things, through piles of books and preconceived ideas. Systematically, ferociously, we sifted through the preconceived ideas. And then, after these long sessions, on these gala days, we went down to the *Coq d'Or* restaurant to devour some stuffed cabbage. The stuffed cabbage made a cracking sound between our strong teen-age teeth. At the neighboring tables, White Russian colonels and shopkeepers from Smolensk went pale with rage as they read the newspapers, during the long retreat of the Red Army during the summer of '41. For us, things were then already quite clear, in practice. But our thinking was in arrears. We had to adjust our thinking to the reality of the summer of '41, which was blindingly clear. Although it may not seem so, it's not easy to adjust one's backward thinking to a reality in full evolution. I had known Michel in *hypokhagne*, that high-pressure preparatory class for *L'Ecole Normale*, and we had remained friends, after I had left school, being unable to reconcile the studious, abstract and totemic life of *hypokhagne* with the necessity for me to earn a living. And Michel had brought along Freiberg, whose father, a German-Jewish university professor, had been a friend of their family, and whom we lost sight of during the exodus of 1940. We called

him von Freiberg zu Freiberg, since his first name was Hans
and we were thinking of the dialogue in Giraudoux. We
experienced everything through books. Later, to tease him
whenever he split hairs, as he sometimes tended to do, I
called Hans an Austro-Marxist. But it was a gratuitous insult, merely to get his goat. The fact is, he was largely
responsible for our refusing to be satisfied with half-truths
in our re-examination of the world's values. Michel was
obsessed by Kantism, as a moth by lamplight. At that time,
this was fairly common among French professors. In fact,
even today, just look around you, talk to people. You'll
meet lots of grocers, barbers, strangers in trains, who are
Kantians without realizing it. But Hans plunged us head-
long into Hegel. Then he triumphantly took from his brief-
case books we had never heard of, books he had picked up
God knows where. We read Masaryk, Adler, Korsch, La-
briola. *Geschichte und Klassenbewusstsein* took us longer,
because of Michel, who didn't want to let go of it, despite
Hans' commentaries elucidating the entire metaphysics im-
plicit in Lukacs' theses. I remember one collection of issues
of the magazine *Unter dem Banner des Marxismus* that
we dissected like fervent scholiasts. Serious matters began
with the tomes of the Marx-Engels-Gesamte-Ausgabe,
which Hans also had, of course, and called the "Mega." At
this point, reality suddenly took charge again. We no
longer met at the rue Blainville. We were traveling in night
trains, on our way to derail night trains. We were going
to the Othe Forest, to the Taboo underground, the para-
chutes opened silkily in the Burgundy night. Since our ideas
were fairly clearly formulated, they fed our daily practice.

The train whistles, and the guy from Semur gives a start.
"What?" he says.
"Nothing," I say.
"You didn't say anything?"
"Not a word," I reply.

"I thought you did," he says.

I heard him sigh.

"Any idea what time it is?" he asks.

"Not the vaguest notion."

"Night," he says, and then he stops.

"What about the night?" I ask him.

"Has it got long to go?"

"It's just started."

"That's true," he says, "it's just started."

Suddenly, at the opposite end of the car, someone screams.

"Here we go," he says.

The screaming stops short. A nightmare, who knows, they must have shaken the guy. When it's something else, fear, it lasts longer. When it's terror screaming, when it's the idea that you're going to die that's screaming, it lasts longer.

"What is the Night of the Bulgarians?" he asks.

"What?"

"You know, the Night of the Bulgarians," he insists.

I didn't think I had talked about the Night of the Bulgarians. I thought that at one point I had merely thought about it. Had I perhaps talked about it? Or else I'm thinking out loud. I must have thought out loud, in the stifling night of the boxcar.

"So?" he says.

"Well, it's a story."

"What kind of story."

"Actually," I say, "it's a ridiculous story. An ordinary story, you won't be able to make head or tail out of it."

"You don't want to tell me?"

"Of course I do. But actually there's not much to tell. It takes place in a train."

"How appropriate," says the guy from Semur.

"That's what made me think of it. Because of the train."

"So what happened?"

He really wants it. Not all that much, really. He wants to make conversation.

"It's not clear. There are some people in a compartment, and then, without rhyme or reason, some of them start to toss the others out the window."

"Damn, that would be great here," says the guy from Semur.

"To toss a few out the window, or be tossed?" I ask him.

"To be tossed, of course. We'd roll on the snow of the embankment, it would be great."

"Well, actually the story is something like that."

"But why Bulgarians?" he immediately wants to know.

"Why not Bulgarians?"

"You're not trying to tell me," says the guy from Semur, "that Bulgarians are exactly common."

"For Bulgarians," I say, "they must be fairly common."

"No, seriously," he replies, "you're not trying to tell me that Bulgarians are more common than Burgundians."

"For Christ's sake, man, in Bulgaria they're more common than Burgundians."

"Who said anything about Bulgaria?" says the guy from Semur.

"Since we're talking about Bulgarians," I argue, "Bulgaria naturally comes to mind."

"Stop trying to confuse me," he says. "Bulgaria I'll go along with. But don't go telling me it's commonplace to find Bulgarians in stories."

"Of course it is, in Bulgarian stories."

"Is this a Bulgarian story?" he asks.

"Actually, it isn't," I have to admit.

"See," he says in a peremptory tone, "it's not even a Bulgarian story and still it's full of Bulgarians. You have to admit that's fishy."

"You'd have preferred Burgundians?"

"And why not!"

"You think there are all that many Burgundians?"

"I couldn't care less. But it would be great. A railway car full of Burgundians who start tossing each other out the window."

"Do you think that happens all the time, Burgundians tossing each other out the train window?" I ask him.

"You're really going too far," says the guy from Semur. "I have nothing against your lousy story full of bloody Bulgarians. If we delved a little deeper, we'd find there's nothing to your Night of the Bulgarians."

He's right. No comeback.

Suddenly there are the lights of a town. The train passes some houses surrounded by gardens. Then, more imposing buildings. There are more and more lights, and the train enters the station. I look at the station clock, and it's nine. The guy from Semur looks at the clock and, obviously, sees what time it is.

"Christ," he says, "it's only nine o'clock."

The train stops. A niggardly, bluish light pervades the station. I remember that pale light, forgotten today. Yet it's a waiting-light I've known and lived with since 1936. It's a light you use while waiting to turn out all the lights. It's a pre-alert light, but one you use when you know the alert is coming.

Later, I remember—that is, I don't yet remember in this German train station, since it hasn't yet happened—later I saw how you had to turn out not only the lights. You also had to turn out the crematorium. The loudspeakers broadcast the communiqués giving the locations of the air strikes over Germany. At night, when the bombers reached a certain proximity, the lights of the camp were turned out. The margin of security wasn't great, the factories had to keep running, the stoppages had to be kept to a minimum. But there was, nevertheless, a point at which the lights were turned out. We remained in the dark, hearing the dark hum of more or less distant planes. But there were times when the crematorium was overworked. The rhythm of the dead is not something you can easily synchronize with the capacity of a crematorium, however well equipped. In such cases, when the crematorium was going full blast, tall orange flames spilled out of the crematorium chimneys in a welter of dense smoke. "To go up in smoke" is an expression of the camps. Watch out for the Scharführer, he's a bastard, if you rub him the wrong way you're as good as gone up in smoke. This or that friend, at the end of his rope in the "Revier," was going to go up in smoke. So the flames spilled out of the square crematorium chimney. Then we heard the voice of the S.S. duty guard in the control tower. We heard his voice coming over the loudspeakers: "Krematorium, ausmachen," he said over and over again. Crematorium, out, crematorium, out. They were obviously upset at having to extinguish the crematorium fires, it lowered production. The S.S. guard was annoyed, he barked the "Krematorium, ausmachen" in a flat, peevish voice. We were seated in the dark, and we could hear the loudspeaker: "Krematorium, ausmachen." "You know what?" said one of the guys, "that means the flames are showing." And then we went on waiting in the dark.

But all that was later. Later in this voyage. For the moment we're in this German train station, and I'm still not familiar with the existence and drawbacks of the crematoriums, on evenings when there are alerts.

There are some people on the station platform, and the name of the station written on a board: TRIER.

"What town is this?" says the guy from Semur.

"Can't you see, it's Trier," I reply.

Oh! for Christ's sake, Je-sus! I said Trier out loud and suddenly I realize. Of course it's Trier, for Christ's sake. Was I blind, my God, deaf, dumb and blind, an oaf, an utter idiot, not to have realized sooner where it was I had heard of the Moselle valley?

"You seem surprised that this is Trier," says the guy from Semur.

"Hell, yes," I answer, "I am surprised."

"Why? You used to know it?"

"No, I mean I've never been here."

"Then you know someone from here?" he asks.

"That's it, yes, that's it."

"So now you've got kraut friends," he says suspiciously.

Now I've got kraut friends, it's as simple as that. The Moselle winegrowers, the Moselle woodcutters, the law about stealing wood in the Moselle. It was in the "Mega," of course. It's a childhood friend, dammit, this damned Moselle is a childhood friend of mine.

"Krauts? Never heard of them, what do you mean by that?"

"Listen, you're going too far," the guy says, "this time you're really going too far."

He seemed annoyed.

There are some people on the station platform, and they have just realized that this is not just another train. They must have seen the silhouettes stirring behind the metal grillwork covering the openings. They're talking among themselves, pointing at the train, they're all excited. There's one kid about ten years old, with his parents, directly opposite our car. He listens to his parents, looks in our direction, shakes his head. Then he dashes off. Then he comes running back with a big stone in his hand. Then he comes over toward us and heaves the stone as hard as he can against the opening we're standing beside. We duck down quickly, the stone ricochets off the barbed wire, it just missed hitting the guy from Semur in the face.

"Still don't know any krauts?" he says.

I remain silent. I'm thinking that it's a goddamn dirty

trick this had to happen at Trier, of all places. There are plenty of other German cities along the way.

"Now do you know the krauts, and the kraut children?" The guy from Semur is gloating.

"That has nothing to do with it."

Just then the train starts off again. On the station platform a ten-year-old kid still stands, shaking his fist at us and screaming arrant nonsense.

"Let me tell you something about the krauts," he says, "there's nothing very special or mysterious about the krauts, believe me."

The train picks up speed and plunges into the night.

"Put yourself in his place."

I'm trying to explain to him.

"In whose place?"

"That kid's," I reply.

"Hell, no," he says. "Let him stay in his own place, the little kraut bastard."

I say nothing, not wanting to become involved in a discussion. I wonder how many Germans will still have to be killed so that this German kid will have a chance not to become a kraut. That kid's not to blame, and yet he's completely to blame. He's not the one who turned himself into a little Nazi, and yet he is a little Nazi. Maybe there's no longer any way for him not to become a little Nazi, no way for him not to grow up and become a full-grown Nazi. On this individual scale, questions are of no interest. Whether this kid ceases being a little Nazi or whether he turns into one is meaningless. Meanwhile, the only thing to do, if this kid is ever to have a chance of not becoming a little Nazi, is to destroy the German army. To go on exterminating lots of Germans, so that they can stop being Nazis, or krauts, to use the basic, brainwashed vocabulary of the guy from Semur. In one sense, that's what the guy from Semur means, in his primitive language. But in another sense, his

language, and the vague ideas his language conveys, pre-
clude any possible discussion of the matter. For if they
really are krauts they'll never be anything else. Their "kraut-
ness" is like an essence that no human act will ever be able
to reach. If they are krauts, they'll always be krauts. It's no
longer a social phenomenon, as it is to be German and
Nazi. It's a reality that hovers above history, against which
one is helpless. There would be no point in destroying the
German army, the survivors would still be krauts. The only
alternative would be to go to sleep and wait for time to
pass. But they're not krauts, obviously. They're Germans,
and often Nazis. A trifle too often right now. Their German
—and all too often Nazi—being is part of a given historical
structure, and it's human practice that resolves such matters.

But I don't say anything to the guy from Semur. I'm in
no mood to get involved in a discussion.

I don't know many Germans. I know Hans. With him
there's no problem. I wonder what Hans is doing now, and
I don't know that he's going to die. He's going to die one
of these nights in the forest up above Chatillon. I know the
boys from the Gestapo too, Dr. Haas with his gold teeth.
But what difference is there between these characters from
the Gestapo and the Vichy cops who interrogated you all
one night at the Central Police Station in Paris, that time
you were so damned lucky. You couldn't believe your eyes
next morning, out in the gray Paris streets. There's no
difference. They're both equally kraut, that is, one is no
more kraut than the other. There may be some slight differ-
ences of degree, method or technique; there's no difference
in kind. I have to explain all that to the guy from Semur,
of course he'll understand.

I also know that German soldier from Auxerre, that
German sentinel in the Auxerre Prison. The small exercise
yards in the Auxerre Prison formed a sort of semicircle.
You arrived by the sentinel's path, the guard opened the

door to the yard, closed it behind you with a key. You remained there, in the autumn sun, with that sound of the key behind you. On either side, smooth walls, high enough to keep you from communicating with the adjoining yards. The space between these walls grew more narrow the farther you went. At the far end there was no more than a yard and a half between the two walls, and this space was enclosed by bars. In this way, the sentinel could see everything that went on in the yards, merely by taking a few steps in one direction or the other.

This particular sentinel, I had noticed, was often on duty. He seemed to be about forty. He paused in front of my yard and watched. I was pacing to and fro, unless it was fro and to, or else I was leaning against the sun-drenched wall of the yard. I was still in solitary, I was alone in my yard. One day during the walk, I remember it was a lovely day, one of the noncommissioned officers from the Joigny Feldgendarmerie suddenly stops next to the bars of my yard. Vacheron was beside him. From messages which had reached me, I had learned that Vacheron had ratted. But he had been picked up at Laroche-Migennes over some other matter, the days were going by and it actually seemed as though he hadn't brought my name into it. The guy from the Feld and Vacheron are standing before my bars, and the sentinel, this sentinel I'm referring to, is a little behind.

"Ach so!" says the guy from the Feld. And he calls me over to the bars.

"You know each other?" he says, pointing first to one then to the other.

Vacheron is two feet away from me. He's nothing but skin and bones, has a beard, his face is marked up. He's doubled over like an old man, and his glance is unsteady.

"No," I say, "never saw him before."

"Of course you did," Vacheron mutters.

"Ach so," says the guy from the Feld, and laughs.

"Never saw him before," I repeat.

Vacheron looks at me and shrugs his shoulders.

"And Jacques?" says the guy from the Feld. "You know Jacques?"

Jacques, of course, is Michel. I think of the rue Blainville. All that is prehistory now. The absolute mind, reifying, objectivism, the dialectic of the master and the slave: that's no more than the prehistory leading up to this living history which includes the Gestapo, the questions asked by the guy from the Feld, and Vacheron. Vacheron is also part of living history. That's my bad luck.

"Which Jacques?" I ask. "Jacques who?"

"Jacques Mercier," says the guy from the Feld.

I shake my head.

"Don't know him," I say.

"Yes you do," Vacheron mutters.

He looks at me and makes a gesture of resignation.

"It's hopeless," he says again.

"Fuck off," I say between clenched teeth.

His face, marked by the Feld, reddens slightly.

"What? What?" shouts the guy from the Feld, who is missing some of the subtleties of the conversation.

"Nothing."

"Nothing," says Vacheron.

"You don't know anyone?" the guy from the Feld asks again.

"No one," I say.

He looks at me, assessing me with his eyes. He gives a smile. He looks like the man who is thinking that he could introduce me to a whole lot of nice people.

"Who's taking care of you?" he asks me now.

"Dr. Haas."

"Ach so," he says.

He seems to feel that if Dr. Haas is taking care of me I

must be well taken care of. Actually, the guy's nothing but an insignificant noncommissioned officer in the Feldgendarmerie and Dr. Haas is the Gestapo chief for the entire region. This guy from the Feld has all due respect for hierarchy, he has no need to worry about one of Dr. Haas' patients. Here we are, on opposite sides of the bars, in the autumn sun, and we look as though we're discussing some illness of mine which Dr. Haas is efficiently treating.

"Ach so," says the guy from the Feld.

And he takes Vacheron away.

I remain standing beside the bars, wondering whether that's going to be the end of it or whether there will be further repercussions. The German sentinel is on the other side of the bars, standing in front of my yard, watching me. I hadn't noticed him approach.

He's a soldier of forty or so, with a heavy face, unless it's the helmet that makes his face look heavy. He has a frank, open expression.

"Verstehen Sie Deutsch?" he asks me.

I tell him yes, I understand German.

"Ich möchte Sie etwas fragen," the soldier says.

The man is polite. He wants to ask me a question, and he's asking my permission to ask it.

"Bitte schön," I tell him.

He's three feet from the bars, he hitches up the strap of his rifle, which had slipped down off his shoulder. The sun is warm, we're being assiduously polite. The thought flits through my mind that maybe the guy from the Feld is telephoning right now to the Gestapo, as a matter of duty. Maybe they'll put two and two together and find that it is indeed strange that I said nothing about Jacques, that I didn't know Vacheron. Maybe the whole thing's going to start all over again.

These thoughts flit through my mind; anyway, there's nothing I can do about it. Besides, it's obvious, one should only worry about soluble problems. The same principle ought to apply on an individual basis as well, which, in fact, is the conclusion we had reached at the *Coq d'Or*.

This German soldier wants to ask me a question, "go right ahead" I tell him, we're polite, it's all very civilized.

"Warum sind Sie verhaftet?" the soldier wants to know. I must say, it's an appropriate question. It's the question which, at this particular moment, goes further than any question possible. Why was I arrested? To answer this question is not only to say who I am, but also who all the others are who are presently being arrested. It's a question that will, with no trouble, project us from the specific to the general. Why was I arrested, that is, why are we being arrested, why are people in general being arrested? What is similar about all these dissimilar people who are getting themselves arrested? What is the historical essence common to all these dissimilar, for the most part innocuous, people who are getting themselves arrested? But this is a question that goes even further. In trying to fathom the reasons for my arrest, we'll come upon the other aspect of the question. I was arrested because someone arrested me, because there are those who arrest and those who are arrested. In asking me: Why were you arrested? he's also, in the same breath, asking: Why am I here guarding you? Why have I been ordered to open fire on you if you should try to escape? In short, who am I? That's what this German is asking. A question pregnant with meaning, in other words.

But obviously I don't tell him all that. It would be too damn ridiculous. I try to explain to him in a few words the reasons that led me here.

"You mean you're a terrorist?" he says.

"That's one way of putting it," I reply, "but that doesn't get us anywhere."

"What doesn't?"

"That word isn't going to get you anywhere."

"I'm trying to understand," the soldier says.

Hans would be pleased to see the progress I've made in his native language. He loved his native language, Hans von Freiberg zu Freiberg did. Not only can I read Hegel, I can also talk with a German soldier in the Auxerre Prison. It's much more difficult to talk with a German soldier than to read Hegel. Especially to talk with him about essentials, about life and death, about the reasons for living and the reasons for dying.

I try to explain to him why the word "terrorist" won't get him anywhere.

"Let's go over it once again, all right?" he says to me when I've finished.

"Let's go over it once again."

"What you want is to defend your country."

"No I don't," I reply, "it's not my country."

"What?" he exclaims. "What isn't your country?"

"France," I tell him. "France isn't my country."

"That doesn't make any sense," he says, taken aback.

"Of course it does. Anyway, I'm defending my country when I defend France, which isn't my country."

"What is your country?"

"Spain."

"But Spain's our friend," he says.

"You think so? Before you fought this war, you fought against Spain, which wasn't your friend."

"I didn't fight any war," he said dully.

"Really?"

"I mean, I didn't want any war," he specified.

"Really?" I repeat.

"I'm sure of it," he said solemnly.

Again he hitches up the strap of his rifle, which had slipped down.

"I'm not the least bit sure."

"Why not?"

He seems hurt that I doubt his word.

"Because you're here with your rifle. Which means you wanted it."

"Where else could I be?" he said glumly.

"You could be shot, you could be in a concentration camp, you could be a deserter."

"It's not so easy as all that," he says.

"Of course it is. It's easy to have yourself interrogated by your compatriots from the Feldgendarmerie or the Gestapo."

He makes a sudden gesture of denial.

"I don't have anything to do with the Gestapo."

"You have everything to do with it," I tell him.

"'Nothing, I swear it," he seems terribly upset.

"Everything, until you prove the contrary," I insist.

"I wouldn't want to, with all my heart I wouldn't want to have anything to do with it."

He seems sincere, he seems terrified at the idea of my putting him in the same category as his compatriots of the Feld or the Gestapo.

"Then why are you here?" I ask him.

"That is the question," he says.

But we hear the key in the lock of the yard, the guard is coming to pick me up.

That, indeed, is the question, *das ist die Frage*. We come to it inevitably, even via this disjointed dialogue between deaf men that has just occurred. And I'm the one who has to ask the question: *Warum sind Sie hier?* because mine is a privileged situation. Privileged with respect to this German soldier and to the questions to be asked. Because the historical essence common to all of us who are being arrested in this year 1943 is freedom. We, who can be so dissimilar, resemble each other, we become identified with one another, to the extent that we partake of this freedom. And it is to the extent that we partake of this freedom that we get ourselves arrested. It's our freedom, therefore, that has to be interrogated, not the fact that we've been arrested or are prisoners. Obviously, I'm excluding the people who traffick in the black market and the mercenaries in the various branches of the resistance. Their common bond is money, not freedom. And, of course, I'm not implying that we all partook equally of that freedom common to us. Some people, and there are certainly a good many of them, partake accidentally of this freedom which is common to us. Perhaps they freely chose the resistance, the clandestine life, but since then they've been living on the initial impulse of that free act. They have freely accepted the necessity of joining the maquis, but since then they've been living in the routine which that free act set in motion. They are not living their freedom, they are ensconced in it. But I won't go into the details or ramifications of this problem here. I mention freedom only in passing; what I'm actually concerned with is the story of this voyage. I merely wanted to say that there is only one possible reply to that question asked by the German soldier from Auxerre: *Warum sind Sie verhaftet?* I'm in prison because I'm a free man, because I found it necessary to exercise my freedom, because I accepted this necessity. Similarly, to the question I asked the German sentinel on that October day: *Warum sind Sie hier?*—which happens to be an even more profound question—to this question there is also one possible reply. He is here because he isn't somewhere else, bcause he did not feel the need to be somewhere else. Because he is not free.

The next day the German soldier came back to the bars, and this disjointed conversation, in the course of which the most momentous questions spontaneously came up, continued.

I think of this soldier from Auxerre because of the kid on the station platform at Trier. The kid himself is not involved. He is only in so far as he has *been* involved, he did not involve himself. He threw the stone at us because that mad, brainwashed society in which he is being raised had to throw the stone at us. For we are the possible negation of that society, of that historical entity, that system which the German nation is today. All of us, together, that ridiculously small percentage of us who are going to survive, are the possible negation of that society. Down with us, shame on us, stones at us. We should not attach too much importance to these things. Of course it was unpleasant, this kid brandishing the stone and spouting arrant nonsense on the station platform. *"Shufte,"* he shouted. *"Banditen."* But we shouldn't attach too much importance to it.

This German soldier from Auxerre I'm thinking of is something else again, however. For he would like to understand. He was born in Hamburg, he lived and worked there, he was often out of work there. And for years now he hasn't understood why he is what he is. There are plenty of respectable philosophers who tell us that life is not a being but a making, or more precisely a self-making. They're pleased with their formula, they have it coming out of their ears, they think they've invented the wheel. Just ask this German soldier I knew in the Auxerre Prison. Just ask this German from Hamburg who was out of work most of the time till the Nazis came along and started up the industrial machine of re-militarization again. Ask him why he hasn't "made" his life, why all he has been able to do is submit to the "being" of his life. His life has always been an overwhelming "fact," a "being" outside himself which he has never been able to take possession of, to make it habitable.

We're on opposite sides of the bars, and never have I understood more clearly why I was fighting. We had to make this man's being habitable, or rather the being of

all men like him, because for him it was no doubt already
too late. We had to make the being of this man's sons habitable, his sons who perhaps were the same age as that kid
who threw the stone at us at Trier. It was no more complicated than that, that is it's really the most complicated
thing in the world. For it's quite simply a question of in-
stituting a classless society. There was no question of doing
it for this German soldier, he was going to live and die in
his being which was uninhabitable, opaque and incomprehensible even to himself.

But the train is moving, leaving Trier behind, and I must
get on with this voyage, I leave behind the memory of this
German soldier from the Auxerre Prison. I've told myself
I would write the story of the Auxerre Prison. A very simple
story: the exercise period, that long conversation, in short
snatches, each of us on our own side of the bars. That is,
I was on my side, he didn't know which side he was on.
And now I have a chance to write that story, and I can't.
The time isn't ripe, my subject is this voyage, and I've al-
ready strayed far enough away from it.

I saw this soldier till the end of November. Less fre-
quently, for it never stopped raining and they suppressed
the exercise period. I saw him at the end of November,
before his departure. I was no longer in solitary confinement, I was sharing a cell with Ramaillet and this young
member of the maquis from the Othe Forest, who had been
in the Hortieux brothers' group. In fact, the night before
they had shot the oldest of the Hortieux brothers. During
the quiet hour preceding the exercise period, The Mouse
had gone up to get the oldest Hortieux brother, who for the
past six days had been in a cell along death row. Through
the half-open door we saw The Mouse go up. At Auxerre
there was a highly practical system of locks, which allowed
the doors to be kept locked even though they were partly
open. They left them like that during winter, except on

days when collective punishment was imposed, so that a little
heat, rising from the big stove on the ground floor, would
come into the cells. The stairway was directly opposite our
door, we had seen The Mouse arrive and heard his steps
fading off to the left, along the inner balcony. The death-
row cells were at the far end of this balcony. Ramaillet was
on his cot. As usual, he was reading one of his tracts on
theosophy. The guy from the Othe Forest came over and
hugged the half-open door beside me. If I remember correctly—and I don't believe this memory has been reshaped
in my mind—a heavy silence fell over the prison. The floor
above, where the women were kept, grew quiet. Also the
balcony across the way. Even that character who was forever singing "My dearest love, my love Saint John," grew
quiet. For days we've been waiting for them to come and
get the oldest Hortieux brother, and now The Mouse is
heading for the cells along death row. We hear the noise
of the lock. The oldest Hortieux brother must be sitting on
his cot, his hands handcuffed, wearing no shoes, and he
hears the noise of the lock, unusual for this time of day.
In any event, the hour of death is always unusual. For several minutes there is nothing but silence, and then we hear
the sound of The Mouse's boots returning. The oldest
Hortieux brother stops in front of our cell; he has on wool
socks, his hands are handcuffed, his eyes are shining. "It's
all over, boys," he says through our half-opened door. We
reach through the crack in the door, we shake the handcuffed hands of the oldest Hortieux brother. "So long,
boys," he says. We don't say a word, we shake hands with
him, we have nothing to say. The Mouse is standing beside the oldest Hortieux brother, he turns his head away.
He doesn't know what to do, he rattles the keys, he looks
away. He looks like a decent family-man, his gray-green
uniform is frayed, his decent family-man head looks away.
There's nothing one can say to a friend who's about to die,

we shake hands with him, we have nothing to say. "René, where are you René?" It's the voice of Philippe Hortieux, the youngest of the Hortieux brothers, who's in solitary in a cell along the balcony across the way. And then René Hortieux turns and shouts in turn: "It's all over, Philippe, I'm leaving, it's all over." Philippe is the youngest of the Hortieux brothers, he managed to get away when the S.S. and the Feld descended on the Hortieux group at dawn in the Othe Forest. An informer had turned them in, the S.S. and the Feld had descended on them without warning, it was all they could do to put up a desperate, last-ditch stand. But Philippe Hortieux had managed to break through the encirclement. For two days he hid in the forest. Then he came out, shot a German motorcyclist who had stopped beside the road and fled toward Montbard on the dead German's motorcycle. For two weeks, Philippe Hortieux's motorcycle kept appearing at the most unexpected places. For two weeks, throughout the entire region, the Germans tracked him down. Philippe Hortieux had a Smith and Wesson, with a long barrel painted red, they had parachuted a number of them to us not long before. He had a Sten machine gun and some grenades and plastic bombs. Philippe Hortieux could have escaped, he knew all the contact points, he could have left the area. But he stayed on. He went from farm to farm, hiding at night, and for two weeks he waged his own personal war. At high noon, under the September sun, he went to the village where this informer who had turned them in lived. He parked his motorcycle on the square in front of the church and set off to look for him, machine gun in hand. All the windows of the houses opened, the doors opened, and Philippe Hortieux headed toward the village café, past a hedgerow of dry, burning eyes. The blacksmith emerged from his shop, the butcher emerged from his, the local policeman paused on the edge of the sidewalk. The peasants removed the cigarettes from their mouths, the women held their children by the hand. No one said a word, that is, one man said simply: "The Germans are out on the road to Villeneuve." And Philippe Hortieux smiled and kept on walking toward the village café. He was smiling, he knew he was going to do something that had to be done, he was walking past a row of desperate, fraternal eyes. The peasants knew that it was going to be a terrible winter for the boys in the maquis, they knew we'd been sold down the river again with that perennially promised, perennially postponed Allied landing. They watched Philippe Hortieux walking, machine gun in hand, and it was they who were walking, machine gun in hand, to see that justice was done. The informer must have felt the weight of the silence that had suddenly fallen over the village. Perhaps he remembered the sound of the motorcycle, heard a few minutes before. He emerged from the café, he was standing in the doorway with his glass of red wine in his hand, he started to shake like a leaf, and he was dead. Then all the windows were closed, all the doors were closed, the village was emptied of all life, and Philippe Hortieux left. For fifteen days, appearing out of nowhere, he fired on the Feld patrols, he attacked German cars with grenades. Today he's in solitary confinement in his cell, his body broken by the Gestapo's clubs, and he shouts: "René, oh René!" And the whole prison began to shout too, to say good-bye to René Hortieux. The women's floor was shouting, the four resistance galleries were shouting, to say good-bye to the oldest Hortieux brother. I don't remember now what we were shouting, something ridiculous no doubt, that had little or nothing to do with that death which was advancing toward the oldest of the Hortieux brothers. "Don't worry, René." "Hang on, René." "We'll get them, René." And above all our voices, the voice of Philippe Hortieux which was shouting over and over: "René, oh René." I remember that Ramaillet, hearing all that noise, jumped up off his cot. "What's going on? he asked, "what's going on?" We told him he was a dumb prick, we told the dumb prick to mind his own business. The whole prison was shouting, and The Mouse was terrified. The Mouse didn't want any trouble, he said: "Los, los!" and shoved René Hortieux toward the stairs.

It was the next day, a pale sun was shining. In the morning the man assigned to distribute the food whispered to us: "René died like a man." Of course, it was an approximate expression, meaningless in a way. For death is personal only for the person himself, that is to the extent it is accepted, embraced, it can be personal for him, and for him only. It was an approximate expression, but it actually meant what it said. It said that René Hortieux had seized this possibility of dying standing up, of facing death and making it his. I had not seen René Hortieux die, and yet it wasn't hard to imagine how he died. At that time, in 1943, we had had enough experience seeing men die to envisage René Hortieux's death.

Later, I saw men die under similar circumstances. Thirty thousand motionless men were assembled on the main square, where roll call was held, and in the middle the S.S. had erected the gallows. It was forbidden to move your head, to lower your eyes. We had to watch this comrade die. We saw him die. Even if we had been allowed to move our heads, even if we had been allowed to lower our eyes, we would have watched this comrade die. Our ravaged looks would have been fixed upon him, would have followed him onto the gallows. There were thirty thousand of us, perfectly aligned, the S.S. loved order and symmetry. The loudspeaker was screaming: "Das Ganze, Stand!" and we heard thirty thousand pairs of heels click to an impeccable attention. The S.S. love impeccable attentions. The loudspeaker was screaming: "Mützen ab!" and thirty thousand prisoners' berets were seized by thirty thousand hands and

slapped against thirty thousand right legs, in a perfect
chorus-like movement. The S.S. are especially fond of perfect chorus-like movements. It was at this point that they
brought in the fellow-prisoner, his hands tied behind his
back, and made him ascend the gallows. The S.S. like order
and symmetry and the beautiful, chorus-like movements of
browbeaten crowds, but they're a sorry lot. They tell us
that they are going to make an example of him, and they
have no idea how true it is, how exemplary the death of
this comrade is. We were watching this twenty-year-old
Russian mount the platform, this boy condemned for sabo-
taging the Mibau works, where the most delicate parts
of the V-1 were manufactured. Standing shoulder to shoulder, by their sheer massive immobility, their inscrutable
gazes, the Soviet prisoners of war were frozen in a mournful attention. We watched this twenty-year-old Russian ascend to the platform, and the S.S. delude themselves into
thinking that we are going to experience his death, feel it
descend upon us like a threat or warning. But we are busy
accepting it for ourselves, if it should come to that. We are
busy choosing it for ourselves. We are busy dying this pal's
death, and by doing so we negate it, we cancel it, from
his death we are deriving meaning and purpose for our
own lives. A perfectly valid plan for living, the only valid
one at the present time. But the S.S. are a sorry lot and
never understand such things.

So there was a pale sun shining, it was the end of November, and I was alone in my prison yard with Ramaillet. The
guy from the Othe Forest had been taken away to be interrogated. That same morning we had had a violent argument with Ramaillet, and Ramaillet was keeping to himself.

The German sentinel was standing against the bars, and
I went over to them.

"Yesterday afternoon?" I asked him.

His face stiffened, and he looked at me intently.

"What do you mean?" he said.

"Were you on duty yesterday afternoon?" I make it more specific.

He shakes his head.

"No," he says, "I didn't take part."

We study each other and say nothing.

"But if you had been chosen?"

He doesn't answer. What can he say?

"If you had been picked," I go on, "would you have taken part in the execution?"

He looks like a trapped animal, and he's having trouble swallowing.

"You would have shot my comrade."

He says nothing. What could he say? He lowers his head, he shuffles his feet on the wet earth, he looks up at me.

"I'm leaving tomorrow," he says.

"Where are you going?"

"To the Russian front," he says.

"Oh, you're going to see what a real war is like."

He looks at me, he shakes his head, his voice is listless.

"You want me to die," he says listlessly.

I want him to die? *Wünsche ich seinen Tod?* I wasn't under the impression I wanted him to die. But in a way he's right, I do hope he'll die.

So long as he goes on being a German soldier, I hope he'll die. So long as he persists in being a German soldier, I hope he experiences the storm of fire and iron, the sweat, blood and tears. I hope to see his German soldier's blood, his Nazi Army blood spilled, I do hope he'll die.

"Don't hold it against me."

"I don't," he says. "That's as it should be."

"I only wish I could feel differently," I tell him.

He gives a weary smile.

"It's too late," he says.

"But why is it?"

"I'm all alone," he says.

There's nothing I can do to break his solitude. Only he could do something, but he hasn't the will. He's forty, his life is already settled, he has a wife and children, no one can choose for him.

"I'll remember our conversations," he says.

And he smiles again.

"I want to wish you all possible happiness."

I look straight at him as I say that.

"Happiness?" and he shrugs his shoulders.

Then he glances around and puts his hand in the pocket of his long cape.

"Here," he says, "as a souvenir."

He quickly hands me through the bars two packs of German cigarettes. I take the cigarettes. I hide them in my jacket. He moves away from the bars and smiles again.

"Maybe," he says, "I'll be lucky. Maybe I'll come out of it."

He's not only thinking of coming out alive. He's thinking of really coming out of it.

"I hope so."

"No you don't," he says. "You hope I'll die."

"I hope the German army will be annihilated. And I hope that you will come out of it."

He looks at me, he shakes his head, he says "Thanks," he tugs on the strap of his rifle and he leaves.

"Are you asleep?" the guy from Semur asks.

"No."

"Thirsty, eh?" says the guy from Semur.

"And how."

"There's a little toothpaste left," says the guy from Semur.

"Let's have it."

This is still another trick the guy from Semur-en-Auxois dreamed up. He must have planned his trip like you plan for a polar expedition. The guy thought of everything. Most people had concealed pieces of sausage, bread, biscuits in their pockets. That was sheer madness, the guy from Semur maintained. The real problem wasn't going to be hunger, he said, but thirst. And sausage, dried biscuits, all these solid foods that the others had concealed would only make them more thirsty. People could go for several days without eating, since in any case they were going to be kept immobilized. The real problem was thirst. So he had concealed a few ripe, juicy little apples and a tube of toothpaste in his pockets. The apples were no great stroke of genius, anyone could have thought of that, given the initial premise that the main enemy would be thirst. But the toothpaste was a stroke of pure genius. You spread a thin layer of toothpaste on your lips, and when you inhaled your mouth was filled with a pleasant, mentholated odor.

The apples were gone long ago, because he shared them with me. He hands me the tube of toothpaste, and I put a little on my dry lips. I hand the tube back to him.

The train is going faster now, almost as fast as a real train that might really be going somewhere.

"Provided it lasts," I say.

"What lasts?"

"The speed," I reply.

"Hell, yes," he says. "I've had about as much as I can take."

The train is moving right along, and the boxcar is a harsh rumble of complaints, muffled cries, conversations. The packed bodies, softened by the night, form a thick jelly which oscillates crazily at every curve in the track. And then, suddenly, there are long moments of heavy silence, as if everyone were simultaneously slipping into the solitude of anxiety, into a nightmarish half-sleep.

"That goddamn Ramaillet," I say, "what a long face he would have made."

"Who's Ramaillet?" the guy from Semur wants to know.

It's not that I want to talk about Ramaillet. But since nightfall I've sensed a subtle change in the guy from Semur. I have a strong hunch he needs someone to talk to. Since nightfall, I've detected something like a crack in his voice. The fourth night of this voyage.

"A guy who was in prison with me," I explain.

Ramaillet had told us that he had furnished provisions to the maquis, but we suspected that he had merely been trafficking in the black market. He was a peasant from the Nuits-Saint-Georges region, and he seemed to be consumed with a passion for theosophy, esperanto, homeopathic medicine, nudism and vegetarian theories. As for this last, it was a purely platonic passion, his favorite dish being roast chicken.

"That bastard," I say to the guy from Semur, "he used to receive enormous food packages and he refused to share them."

Actually, when we were alone in the cell, just the two of us, before the guy from the Othe Forest arrived, he didn't refuse to share them. For the question was never raised. How would I have dared ask him to give me anything? It was inconceivable for me to ask him such a question. Therefore he didn't refuse to share. He simply didn't share. We used to eat the greasy, dubious soup in our metal mess tins. We were seated facing each other on our metal camp beds. We ate the soup without saying a word. I made it last as long as possible. I took tiny spoonfuls of the insipid broth, which I forced myself to enjoy. I pretended to be saving for later the rare pieces of solid matter that occasionally trailed in the insipid broth. But it was hard to cheat, it was hard to make the soup last. I used to tell myself stories, to make myself eat more slowly. In a low voice I would recite Valéry's *Le Cimetière marin*, trying not to forget anything. But I couldn't do it. Between the line, "All goes underground and re-enters the game," and the end, there was a blank in my memory I couldn't fill. Between, "All goes underground and re-enters the game," and, "the wind is rising, we must try to live," I couldn't for the life of me fill in that blank in my memory. I sat with my spoon suspended in mid-air and tried to remember. Sometimes people ask why I suddenly begin to recite *Le Cimetière marin* when I'm tying my tie or opening a bottle of beer. That's why. In that prison cell at Auxerre, I often recited *Le Cimetière marin,* sitting across from Ramaillet. And that's the only time *Le Cimetière marin* served some useful purpose. That's the only time that distinguished idiot, Valéry, served some useful purpose. But it was impossible to cheat. Even "The assault in the sun of the women's chalk-white bodies" did not allow cheating. There was always too little soup. There was always a point at which the soup was finished. There was no more soup, there had never been any soup. I looked at the empty mess tin, I scraped the empty mess tin, but it was hopeless. Ramaillet, though, gobbled up his soup. For him, the soup was merely a distraction. Under his bed he had two big boxes filled with food that was considerably more substantial. He gulped down his soup and then he belched. "Excuse me," he used to say, covering his mouth with his hand. And then: "It's good for you." Every day, after the soup, he belched. "Excuse me," he would say, "it's good for you." Every day the same thing. You had to hear him belch, say "excuse me, it's good for you," and control your temper. Above all, control your temper.

"I would have strangled him," says the guy from Semur.

"Of course," I reply. "I would have been delighted to."

"And it was after the soup that he would gorge himself?"

"No, it was at night."

"What do you mean, at night."

"I mean, at night."

"But why at night?" the guy from Semur wants to know.

"When he thought I was asleep."

"Oh, shit," he says, " I would have strangled him."

One had to control one's temper, above all one had to control one's temper, it's a question of dignity.

He used to wait till I was asleep, at night, to devour his provisions. But I wasn't asleep, or else hearing him stir used to wake me up. I lay there motionless in the dark, and I could hear him eating. I could barely make out his silhouette on the bed, and I could hear him eating. From the sound of his jaws, I gathered he was eating chicken, I could hear the little bones of the well-cooked chicken cracking. I could hear the biscuits cracking between his teeth, not the grating, sandy cracking of dried biscuits, no, it was a muffled cracking, muffled by the layer of Swiss cheese I could picture spread on the biscuit. I could hear him eating, my heart was beating, and I forced myself to control my temper. Ramaillet used to eat at night because he didn't want to yield to the temptation of sharing the slightest scrap with me. If he had eaten during the day, sooner or later he would have yielded. Seeing me there before him, watching him eat, who knows, perhaps he would have yielded to the temptation and given me a small chicken bone or a little piece of cheese. But that would have created a precedent. And as the days went by, it might have become a habit. Ramaillet was wary of that possibility. Because I never used to receive any packages, and there wasn't the slightest possibility that I would ever be able to repay him a chicken bone or piece of cheese. So he used to eat at night.

"I never imagined such a thing was possible," says the guy from Semur.

"Anything is possible."

He grunts in the dark.

"You," he says, "always have a ready-made answer for everything."

"But it's true."

I feel like laughing. This guy from Semur is just too comforting for words.

"So? It's true, anything is possible. I still never would have thought such a thing was possible, a thing like that."

For the guy from Semur, there wasn't a moment's hesitation. He had six ripe, juicy apples and he gave me three. That is, he split each of the six apples in two and he gave me six halves of six juicy little apples. That was what had to be done, for him there was no problem. The same was true for the guy from the Othe Forest. When he received his first food package, he said: "All right, let's divide it up." I warned him that I would never have anything to divide. He told me to stop bothering him. "All right, so I bother you, but I just wanted to warn you." "We've had about enough of your lip, right? Now, then, let's divide it up." That was when he suggested to Ramaillet that we put all the food together and divide it into three portions. But Ramaillet said that wouldn't be fair. They were both going to give up a third of their packages so that I could eat as much as they did, and I wasn't contributing anything to the common fund. He said it wouldn't be fair. The guy from the Othe Forest began calling him every name in the book— exactly what the guy from Semur would have done. Finally, he told him to fuck off with his fat fucking package, and he shared with me. The guy from Semur would have done the same.

Later on, I saw people steal a piece of black bread from a pal. When a man's survival actually hangs on that thin slice of bread, when his life is hanging by this blackish thread of wet bread, to steal this piece of black bread is to send a comrade to his death. To steal this piece of bread is to choose another man's death to assure your own life, or at least improve your own possibilities. And yet bread was stolen. I saw people grow pale and collapse when they realized that their piece of bread had been stolen. And it was not only a wrong that had been done to them directly. It was an irreparable wrong that had been done to all of us. For suspicion settled in, and distrust and hate. Any one of us could have stolen that piece of bread, we were all guilty. Every theft of bread made each of us a potential bread thief. In the camps, man becomes that animal capable of stealing a mate's bread, of propelling him toward death.

But in the camps man also becomes that invincible being capable of sharing his last cigarette butt, his last piece of bread, his last breath, to sustain his fellow man. That is, man doesn't become that invincible animal in the camps. He already is. It's always been a part of his nature, an inherent possibility. But the camps are extreme situations in which the cleavage between the men and the others is more pronounced. Actually, we didn't need the camps to understand that man is a being capable of the most noble as well as the basest acts. How banal can you get!

"And that's all there is to that story?" asks the guy from Semur.

"Yes, that's all."

"And Ramaillet went on eating his packages all by himself?"

"Of course he did."

"You should have forced him to share," says the guy from Semur.

"That's easy to say," I retort. "He didn't want to, what could we do about it?"

"I still say you should have made him share. When there are three guys in a cell and two agree on something, there are a thousand ways of persuading the third."

"Of course there are."

"So? It seems to me you and the guy from the Othe Forest weren't very much on the ball."

"We never posed the question in those terms."

"And why not?"

"I suppose because the food would have stuck in our throats."

"What food?" the guy from Semur wants to know.

"The food we would have forced Ramaillet to give us."

"Not *give* you. Share with you. You should have made him share everything, his packages and the packages belonging to the guy from the Othe Forest."

"We never posed the problem in those terms," I admit.

"You're just too too tactful, both of you," says the guy from Semur.

Four or five rows behind us there is a violent eddy and the sound of cries.

"What is it now?" says the guy from Semur.

The mass of bodies sways back and forth.

"Air, give him some air," a voice behind us shouts.

"Make some room, for God's sake, so we can move him to the window," a second voice calls out.

The mass of bodies sways, creates an opening, and the shadowy arms of that shadowy mass propel the inanimate body of an old man toward the window and toward us. The guy from Semur has him on one side, I have him on the other, and we're holding him in the cold night air streaming in through the aperture.

"Jesus!" says the guy from Semur. "He looks terrible."

The old man's face is a contracted mask, his eyes are glazed. His mouth is twisted with pain.

"What can we do?" I ask.

The guy from Semur looks at the old man's face and he doesn't reply. The old man's body suddenly contracts. Life flows back into his eyes, and he stares at the night before him.

"What do you know about that?" he says, his voice low but distinct. Then his eyes again falter, and his body slumps into our arms.

"Hey, friend," says the guy from Semur, "don't give up."

But I gather that he's given up for all eternity.

"It must have been some heart thing," says the guy from Semur.

As if knowing what this old man died from was any comfort. Because the old man is dead, beyond all shadow of a doubt. He opened his eyes, he said: "What do you know about that?" and he died. We're holding a corpse in our arms, in the current of cold night air streaming in through the opening.

"He's dead," I tell the guy from Semur.

He knows it as well as I do, but he's slow to admit it to himself.

"It must have been some heart thing," he says again.

It's normal for old men to have a heart condition. But we're twenty, there's nothing wrong with our hearts. That's what the guy from Semur means. He's classifying this old man's death among the unpredictable but logical accidents that befall old men. It's a reassuring thought. This death becomes something not directly related to us. This death has been wending its way into the old man's body, for a long time it has been wending its way. We know how it is with heart attacks, how they strike at any time and any place. But we're twenty, and this kind of death doesn't affect us.

We're holding the corpse in our arms and don't know quite what to do with it.

"How is he?" a voice from behind us calls out.

"He isn't," I reply.

"What?" the voice says.

"He's dead," says the guy from Semur, dispelling any doubt.

A heavy silence settles down. The axles are squeaking around the curves, the train is blowing its whistle, it's still moving along at a good clip. The silence deepens.

"He must have had something wrong with his heart," says another voice out of the heavy silence.

"Are you sure he's dead?" says the first voice.

"Quite sure," says the guy from Semur.

"There's no pulse?" the voice insists.

"No, friend, none," says the guy from Semur.

"How did it happen?" a third voice asks.

"The way it usually does," I reply.

"What does that mean," says the third voice with a trace of irritation.

"It means he was alive and then a second later he was dead," I explain.

"He must have had something wrong with his heart," the same voice as before says again.

There is a short silence, while the men ponder that comforting thought. It's a banal accident, a heart attack, it could have happened to him along the banks of the Marne while he was out fishing. The idea of a heart attack is a comforting one. Except, of course, for those who have heart conditions.

"What'll we do with him?" asks the guy from Semur.

Because we're still holding the corpse by its lifeless arms, holding it toward the cold night air.

"Are you really sure he's dead?" the first voice insists.

"Say, why don't you knock it off," says the guy from Semur.

"Maybe he simply passed out," the voice says.

"Oh, hell," says the guy from Semur, "come over here and see for yourself."

But no one comes. Since we've said that the old man is dead, the mass of bodies nearest us has edged away. It's hardly discernible, but it has edged away. The surrounding mass of bodies is no longer glued to us, it no longer pushes against us with the same force. Like the retractile organism of an oyster, the mass of bodies has flowed back into itself. We no longer feel the same thrust against our shoulders and backs and legs.

"Listen, my friend and I aren't going to hold him all night," says the guy from Semur.

"We have to ask the Germans to stop," says a new voice.

"What for?" someone asks.

"So they can take the body and send it back to his family," says the new voice.

There's a burst of shrill, slightly coarse laughter.

"There's another one who's seen von Stroheim and Jean Gabin in *The Grand Illusion,* in living color," says a voice with a Parisian accent.

"Come on," the guy from Semur says to me, "let's set him down, we'll lay him down against the wall in the corner. He'll take up the least room there."

To translate his words into action, we start to move and, naturally, jostle the people around us.

"Hey, what are you doing?" a voice shouts.

"We're going to set him down on the floor, over in the corner," says the guy from Semur. "That's where he'll take up the least room."

"Watch your step," the guy says, "the pisscan's over there."

"Well, then, push the pisscan out of the way," says the guy from Semur.

"Hell, no," someone else says, "you're not going to stick that pisscan under my nose."

"That's enough out of you," shouts a third voice, filled with rage. "Till now I'm the one who's had your shit under my nose."

"Yours too," says another voice, jokingly.

"I've been holding mine," the previous voice says.

"That's bad for your health," the joker says.

"Will all you guys shut your big mouths," says the guy from Semur. "Move that damn pisscan so we can set this guy down."

"Nobody's going to move that pisscan," says the same guy as a while back.

"And how we're going to move it!" shouts the one who's had the pisscan under his nose till now.

We can hear the noise of the can scraping over the wooden floor. We hear some swearing, a chorus of confused shouts. Then the metallic clatter of the pisscan cover, which must have fallen off.

"Oh, the bastards!" another voice shouts.

"What's the matter?"

"Those smart alecks managed to turn over the pisscan," someone explains.

"No they didn't," says the guy who claims to have had the can under his nose till now, "it's just a trickle."

"Yeah, well I have your trickle on my feet," says the previous voice.

"You can wash your feet when you arrive," says the same joker.

"You think you're funny," says the one who has the trickle on his feet.

"I am," the other one says coolly, "I'm a real clown."

We hear some scattered laughter, a few doubtful cracks and muffled protests. But the pisscan, more or less overturned, has been moved and we can set down the old man's body.

We wedge the corpse against the wall of the boxcar, on its side. In any case, he was so thin he's not going to take up too much room.

The guy from Semur and I stand up, and silence again settles down on us.

He had said: "What do you know about that?" and he had died. What was the "that" he was referring to? He would have had a hard time saying, no doubt. He meant: What do you know about that, meaning: what a life, this life of ours. What do you know about that, meaning: what a world, this world. I know, of course I know. That's all I've been doing, trying to know and let others know. That's really what I want. Through the years, I've often seen this same expression of absolute amazement, the same expression this old man who was going to die had, just before he died. In fact, I admit I have never fully understood why so many guys were so amazed. Perhaps it's because I've grown more used to death on the roads, to crowds trudging along the roads with death at their heels. Perhaps I don't find that amazing because, since July, 1936, I've seen nothing but that. Sometimes all these amazed people get on my nerves. They return dumbfounded from the interrogation. "What do you know about that, they beat the shit out of me!" "But for Christ's sake, what did you expect them to do? You mean to say you didn't know they were Nazis?" They would shake their heads, they didn't know what was happening to them. "But damn it, didn't you know who you were dealing with?" These simple souls sometimes grate on my nerves. Perhaps because I saw the German and Italian fighter planes sweep in low over the roads and calmly machine-gun the crowds, on the roads of my own country. That little wagon with the woman in black and the baby crying is mine. That donkey, and the grandmother on the donkey, is mine. That fiancée, all fire and snow walking down the burning road like a princess, is yours. Maybe all these amazed souls get on my nerves because of the entire villages in exodus on the roads of my country, fleeing from these same S.S. troops, or their equals, their brothers. So, to that question: "What do you know about that?" I have a ready-made answer, as the guy from Semur would say. Yes, I know, that's all I do know. I know, and I'm trying to let others know, which is my purpose here.

We had left the large room where they had made us undress. It was as hot as a steam room, our throats were parched, we were so tired we could scarcely walk. We had run down a hallway, our bare feet were slapping against the cement. Then there was another, smaller room into which the men were crammed as they arrived. At the far end of the room were ten or twelve men in white smocks, with electric clippers whose long wires were suspended from the ceiling. They were sitting on stools and looked bored to death, and they shaved us everywhere there was any hair. The prisoners awaited their turn, jammed in against each other, not knowing what to do with their bare hands against their naked bodies. The shavers worked quickly, it was easy to see they had plenty of experience. They shaved their men in a trice, and it was: All right, next. Pushed and pulled from side to side by the surges of the crowd, I finally reached the front row, directly in front of the shavers. My left shoulder and hip hurt where I had been clubbed a short while before. Beside me were two little old, somewhat misshapen men. In fact, their eyes were bulging with that expression of surprise and disbelief. They were watching this circus, their eyes bulging with disbelief. Their turn came, and they began to squeal when the electric clippers went to work on their sensitive parts. They exchanged glances, and their expression was no longer one of simple amazement but of holy indignation. "What do you know about that, my dear Minister, now what do you know about that?" said one of them. "It's unbelievable, my dear Senator, pos-i-tive-ly unbelievable," the other replied. That's how he said "positively," enunciating each syllable. They had a Belgian accent, they were grotesque, they were abject. I would have liked to hear what the guy from Semur might have had to say about them. But the guy from Semur was dead, he had remained behind in the boxcar. I won't have his thoughts on anything any more.

"This night will never end," says the guy from Semur.

It's the fourth night, don't forget, the fourth night of this voyage. The feeling returns that perhaps we're the ones who are motionless. Perhaps it's the night that moves, the world that unfolds around our gasping immobility. This feeling of unreality grows, it spreads through my body, my bone-weary body, like gangrene. In the past, with the help of cold and hunger, I have easily managed to induce this state of unreality within myself. I used to go down to the Boulevard Saint Michel, to that bakery on the corner of the rue de l'Ecole de Médecine where they sold little buckwheat cakes. I would buy four of them, that was my lunch. With the help of the cold and hunger, it was child's play to incite my ardent brain to the very limits of hallucination. A child's play that came to naught, of course. Today it's different. It's not I who am the cause of this sense of unreality. It's engraved in the external events. It's engraved in the events of this voyage. Fortunately, there was that Moselle interlude, that gentle, shadowy and tender, snow-covered, burning certainty of the Moselle. It was there that I rediscovered myself, that I once again became what I am, what man is, a natural human being, the result of a long history of solidarity and violence, of human defeats and conquests. Since the same set of circumstances has never recurred, I have never again re-experienced the intensity of that moment, that quiet, savage joy in the Moselle valley, that human pride in the presence of this man-made landscape. Sometimes the memory recurs when I see the pure, uneven line of an urban skyline, or the gray sky over a gray plain. And yet this feeling of unreality I experienced during the fourth night of this voyage was not as strong as the one I experienced upon my return from this voyage. The months of prison had doubtless created a kind of familiarity. The unreal and the absurd became familiar. In order to survive, the organism has to adhere closely to reality, and reality was actually this totally *un*natural world of the prison of death. But the real shock occurred when I returned from this voyage.

The two automobiles stopped in front of us, and out of them stepped these incredible girls. It was April 13th, two days after the end of the camps. The beech trees were rustling in the spring breeze. The Americans had disarmed us, it was the first thing they had done, I must say. You would have thought they were frightened to death of these few hundred armed skeletons, these Russian and German, Spanish and French, Polish and Czech skeletons out on the roads around Weimar. But none the less we were occupying the S.S. barracks, the Totenkopf division warehouses, where we had to take inventory. There was an unarmed guard stationed before each building. I was on guard in front of the S.S. officers' building, and the men were smoking and singing. We were no longer armed, but we were still living on the momentum of the previous evening's joy when we had marched out toward Weimar firing on isolated groups of S.S. troops in the woods. I was in front of the S.S. officers' building and these two cars stopped beside us and these incredible girls climbed out. They were wearing well-cut blue uniforms, with a collar patch that said French Mission. They had hair, lipstick, silk stockings. They had legs in the silk stockings, lips alive beneath the lipstick, faces alive below the hair, below their real honest-to-god hair. They were laughing, they were chatting away, it was a real picnic. Suddenly the guys remembered they were men and began to hover around these girls. The girls were simpering, they were chattering, they deserved a couple of good slaps. But these dolls wanted to visit the camp, they had heard that it was horrible, absolutely appalling. They wanted to experience that horror. I took unfair advantage of my authority to leave the other guys where they were in front of the S.S. officers' barracks, and I took these living dolls toward the camp entrance.

The big square where they had held roll call was deserted beneath the spring sun, and I stopped, my heart beating. I had never seen it empty before, I must admit, I hadn't ever really seen it. I hadn't really seen it before, not what you call "seeing." In the distance, from one of the barracks across the way, there floated the slow tune of some song played on an accordion. There was that infinitely fragile accordion tune, there were the tall trees above the barbed wire, there was the wind in the beeches and the April sun above the wind and the beeches. I saw this scenery, which for two years had been the setting of my life, and I was seeing it for the first time. I was seeing it from the outside, as if this setting which had been my life until the day before yesterday was now on the other side of the mirror. There was only that accordion tune linking my former life, my life for two years until the day before yesterday, to my life today. That accordion tune, played by a Russian in that barracks across the way, because only a Russian can entice that fragile, powerful music from an accordion, that trembling of the birches in the wind and the wheat in the endless plains. That accordion tune was the link between my life these past two years, it was like a farewell to that life, like a farewell to all the men, all the friends who had died in the course of that life. I paused on the large empty square where they had held roll call and the wind was in the beeches and the April sun above the wind and the beeches. There was also, off to the right, the squat crematorium building. To the left, there was also the manège where they executed the officers, the commissars and the Communists of the Red Army. Yesterday, April 12th, I had visited the manège. It was just another manège, like any other, the S.S. officers used to come there to ride. The S.S. officers' wives used to come there to ride. But, in the building where one dressed there was also a special shower. A Soviet officer was taken into it, he was given a piece of soap and a bath towel and he waited for the water to flow from the shower. But the water didn't flow. Through a loophole concealed in the corner, an S.S. would send a bullet into the Soviet officer's head. The S.S. was in an adjoining room, he calmly aimed at the Soviet officer's head, and he sent a bullet into his head. They removed the corpse, they gathered up the soap and the bath towel, and they turned on the shower to erase any trace of blood. When you have understood this simulacrum of the shower and the piece of soap, you will have understood the S.S. mentality.

But there's no point trying to understand the S.S.; it suffices to exterminate them.

I was standing on the large empty square, it was April, and I had lost all desire to have these girls in their neat stockings, with their blue skirts clinging fetchingly to their thighs, come and visit my camp. I had completely lost my desire. That accordion tune in the April warmth was not for them. I simply wanted them to get the hell out.

"But it really doesn't seem all that bad," one of them said just then.

The cigarette I was smoking tasted terrible, and I made up my mind to show them something after all.

"Follow me," I said to them.

And I started to walk toward the crematorium building.

"Is that the kitchen?" another girl asked.

"You'll see," I replied.

We are walking across the big square where roll call used to be held, and the accordion tune is fading in the distance.

"This night will never end," says the guy from Semur.

We are standing up, crushed, in the night that will never end. Because of the old man who died saying: "What do you know about that?" we can't move our feet, I mean we can't step on him. I won't tell the guy from Semur that all nights must end, he's liable to haul off and hit me if I do. Besides, it wouldn't be true. Right now, at this precise moment, this night never will end. At this precise moment, the fourth night of the voyage will never end.

I spent the first night of the voyage reconstructing *Swann's Way* in my mind, and it was an excellent exercise in abstraction. For a long time, I too used to go to bed early. I imagined the metallic sound of the bell in the garden on evenings when Swann came to dinner. In my mind's eye, I again saw the colors of the stained glass window of the village church. And that hawthorne hedge, Lord, that hawthorne hedge was my childhood too. I spent the first night of this voyage reconstructing *Swann's Way* in my mind and recalling my childhood. I asked myself whether there wasn't something in my childhood comparable to that phrase of the Vinteuil sonata. Unfortunately, there was nothing. Today, by forcing a little, I suspect there would be something comparable to that phrase of the Vinteuil sonata, to Antoine Roquentin's painful reaction when he heard *Some of these Days.* Today, there would be that melody from *Summertime,* the very beginning of *Summertime* as played by Sidney Bechet. Today, there would also be that incredible moment in that old song from my homeland, a song whose words would translate roughly:

I walk by the bridge
I walk by the river,
I find you always washing there.
The limpid waters bear
Away the colors of your hair.

And it's after these words that the melody I'm referring to begins, painfully pure. But during the first night of this voyage I discovered nothing in my memory that was comparable to the Vinteuil sonata. Later, years later, Juan brought me back from Paris the three small *Pléiade* volumes bound in buckram. I must have spoken to him about the book. "You must have spent a fortune," I said. "It's not that," he said, "but what decadent taste." We both laughed, I poked fun at his mathematician's severity. We laughed, and he went on insistently: "Come on now, admit it's decadent." And I asked him: "What about *Sartoris*?" because I knew he was fond of Faulkner. "And *Absalom, Absalom*?" We settled the question by deciding that it was not a vital one.

"Hey, pal," says the guy from Semur, "you still awake?"
"Yes."
"I've had about as much as I can take."
Me too. No argument there. My right knee hurts more and more and is swelling visibly. That is, when I touch it I can feel that it's swelling visibly.
"You have any idea where the camp we're going to is?" the guy from Semur wants to know.
"Not the slightest."
We're there trying to imagine where it can be, what this camp we're going to will be like.
Now I know. Once I entered that camp, I lived there for two years and now I'm there again, with these incredible girls. I now maintain that they are incredible insofar as they are real, insofar as they are what girls are, in reality. But

the guy from Semur will never know exactly what this camp we're going to is like, this camp we're trying to picture in the depths of the fourth night of this voyage.

I take the girls into the crematorium by the small door, the one leading directly to the cellar. They've just realized it's not a kitchen, and they suddenly fall silent. I show them the hooks from which the men were hung, for the crematorium cellar also served as a torture chamber. I show them the blackjacks and the clubs, which are still there. I explain to them what they were used for. I show them the lifts which used to take the corpses to the second story, to directly in front of the ovens. We go up to the second story and I show them the ovens. The poor girls are speechless. They follow me, and I show them the row of electric ovens, and the half-charred corpses which are still inside. I hardly speak to them, merely saying: "Here you are, look there" It's essential for them to see, to try and imagine. They say nothing, perhaps they are imagining. Perhaps even these young women from the chic district of Passy, from the French Mission, are capable of imagining. I take them out of the crematorium into the interior courtyard surrounded by a high fence. There I say nothing, I let them look. In the middle of the courtyard is a pile of corpses a good twelve feet high. A pile of twisted, yellowed skeletons, their faces hideous with terror. Now the accordion is playing a frenzied "gopak" which floats faintly over to us. The joy of the "gopak" reaches us, it dances over this pile of skeletons which they haven't had time yet to bury. They're in the process of digging the trench into which quicklime will be poured. The frenzied rhythm of the "gopak" dances above these dead of the final day, which have not been removed because the S.S. let the crematorium fires die out when they fled. I'm thinking that in the barracks of the Little Camp the elderly, the ill and the Jews are still dying. For them, the end of the camps will not be the end of death. Looking at these wasted bodies, with their protruding bones, their sunken chests, these bodies piled twelve feet high in the crematorium courtyard, I'm thinking that these were my comrades. I'm thinking that one has to have experienced their death, as we have, in order to look at them with that pure, fraternal expression. In the distance I can hear the joyful rhythm of the "gopak" and I tell myself that these girls from Passy have no business here. It was stupid to try and explain to them. Later, a month from now, in fifteen years, maybe I'll be able to explain all this to anyone. But today, in the April sun, amid these rustling beeches, these dreadful, fraternal dead need no explanation. They need a pure, fraternal look. What they need, quite simply, is for us to live, to live as fully as we can.

I have to get these young ladies from Passy out of here.

I turn around and find them gone. They've fled from this spectacle. I must say I sympathize with them, it can't be much fun to arrive in a beautiful car, wearing a beautiful uniform that hugs the thighs, and stumble onto this pile of hardly presentable corpses.

I emerge onto the square and light a cigarette.

One of the girls is still there, waiting for me. A brunette, with light eyes.

"Why did you do that?" she says.

"It was stupid," I admit.

"But why?"

"You wanted to visit the place," I reply.

"I'd like to see more."

I glance at her. Her eyes are shining, her lips trembling.

"I don't have the strength," I tell her.

She looks at me in silence.

Together we walk toward the entrance to the camp. A black flag is flying at half-mast from the control tower.

"Is that for the dead?" she asks, her voice trembling.

"No. That's for Roosevelt. The dead don't need a flag."

"What do they need?" she asks.

"A pure, fraternal look," I reply. "And to be remembered."

She looks at me and says nothing.

"Good-bye," she says.

"So long." And I rejoin the boys.

"This night, Jesus, this night will never end," says the guy from Semur.

I saw that dark-haired girl again at Eisenach, a week later. A week or two weeks, I can't remember. For that was a week or two that passed like a dream, between the end of the camps and the start of life as it was before. I was sitting on the grass of some lawn, outside the barbed-wire enclosure, in among the S.S. houses. I was smoking and listening to the varied sounds of spring. I was looking at the blades of grass, the insects on the blades of grass. Suddenly there was Yves running toward me. He had just arrived from Eisenach with a French Army truck. A three-truck convoy was leaving the next day directly for Paris, he had reserved me a seat, and had come from Eisenach to pick me up. I look at the camp. I see the watchtowers, the barbed wires through which electric current no longer runs. I see the buildings of the D.A.W., the zoological garden where the S.S. used to raise deer, monkeys and bears.

All right, I'm going. There's nothing I have to get, I can leave as I am. I have Russian boots with soft tops, striped trousers of coarse cloth, a shirt from the Wehrmacht, and a gray wool sweater with green facings on the collar and sleeves and, on the back, large letters painted in black: KL BU. All right, I'm going. It's over. I'm leaving. I hope Hans and Michel are alive. I don't know that Hans is dead. I hope that Julien is alive. I don't know that Julien is dead.

I throw away my cigarette, I crush it under my heel on the grass of the lawn, I'm going to leave. This voyage is over, I'm going back, I'm not going home, but I'm getting closer. The end of the camps is the end of Nazism, which means the end of Franco, obviously, beyond all shadow of a doubt. I'll be able to worry about serious matters, as Piotr would say, now that the war is over. I wonder what sort of serious matters I'm going to worry about. Piotr had said: "Rebuild my factory, go to the movies, beget children."

I run with Yves to the truck, and we're speeding along the road to Weimar. All three of us—Yves, the driver and I —are sitting on the front seat. Yves and I spend our time pointing out things to each other. Look, the Politische Abteilung barracks. Look, Ilse Koch's house. Look, the station, that's where we arrived. Look, the buildings of the Mibau works. Then there was nothing else to look at except the road and the trees, the trees and the road, and we sang. That is Yves and the driver sang. I only pretended to, because I can't for the life of me carry a tune.

Here's the curve where, at noon on the 11th of April, we ran into a group of retreating S.S. The Spaniards, with a group of Panzerfaust and a group armed with automatic weapons, were advancing down the main axis of the road. The French to the left and the Russians to the right. The S.S. had a half-track and they were fleeing down a forest trail into the woods. Off to our right, we heard the commander's shouts and then, three times in a row, a long "hurrah." The Russians charged at the S.S. with grenades and bayonets. The rest of us, the French and Spanish, maneuvered to outflank the S.S. and overrun them. What ensued is that chaotic thing known as combat. The half-track burst into flame, and suddenly there was total silence. That chaotic thing called combat was over. We were in the process of regrouping our forces on the road when I saw two

young Frenchmen arrive with a wounded member of the
S.S. I knew them slightly, they were partisans from my
own section.

"Hey Gérard," they called out as they approached. In
those days, my name used to be Gérard.

The S.S. man was wounded in the shoulder or the arm.
He was holding his wounded arm and looked terrified.

"We have this prisoner, Gérard, what'll we do with him?"
one of them said.

I look at the S.S. man. I know him. A Blockführer who
was forever screaming and persecuting the prisoners. I
looked at the two young Frenchmen, I was on the verge of
saying: "Shoot him on the spot and rejoin your group, we're
going on," but the words stuck in my throat. Because I have
just realized that they'll never do it. I've just read in their
eyes that they'll never do it. They're twenty years old,
they're embarrassed by this prisoner, but they're not going
to shoot him. I know that, historically speaking, this is an
error. I know that with an S.S. man, dialogue becomes
possible only after he is dead. I know that the problem is
to modify the historical structure which permits the appearance of the S.S. But once the S.S. man is there, one has
no choice but to exterminate him whenever the occasion
arises in the course of battle. I know that these two young
men are going to do something foolish, but I'm not going
to stop them.

"What do you think about it?" I asked them.

They exchange glances and shake their heads.

"The bastard's wounded," one of them says.

"That's right," the other one says. "He's wounded, first
we have to take care of him."

"So?" I ask them.

They look at each other. They also know they're going to
do something foolish, but still they're going to do it. They

remember their comrades who were tortured or shot. They remember the Kommandatur's posters, the execution of hostages. Perhaps it was in their section that the S.S. cut off the hands of a three-year-old child to force its mother to talk, to make her denounce a resistance group. The mother saw both her child's hands cut off and she didn't talk, she went mad. They know that they're going to do something foolish. But they didn't volunteer for and fight this war in order to execute a wounded prisoner. They fought this war against Fascism, so that wounded prisoners would no longer be executed. They know that they're going to do something foolish, but they're going to do it consciously. And I'm going to let them.

"We're going to take him to camp," one of them says, "so they can take care of the bastard."

He emphasizes the term "bastard" to make me clearly understand that they're not going soft, that they're not committing this foolish act out of weakness.

"All right," I say. "But leave your rifles with me. We're short of guns here."

"Come on, now," says one of them, "that's going a little far."

"I'll give you a parabellum in exchange, to take in this character. But you're going to leave me your rifles, I need them."

"You'll give them back to us, won't you?"

"Of course, as soon as you've rejoined the column I'll give them back to you."

"No joke, now," they say.

"No joke," I assure them.

"You wouldn't do that to us, I mean leave us without a rifle?"

"Of course I wouldn't."

We effect the exchange, and they prepare to leave. The

S.S. man has been following the conversation, looking like a trapped animal. He's fully aware that his fate is hanging in the balance. I look at him.

"Ich hätte Dich erschossen," I tell him. I would have shot you.

He looks at me imploringly.

"Aber die beiden hier sind zu jung, sie wissen nicht dass Du erschossen sein solltest. Also, los, zum Teufel." But these two guys are too young, they don't realize you ought to be shot, I told him. And then I told him to go to hell.

They set off. I watch them go, and I know that we've done something foolish. But I'm happy that these two young partisans have committed this foolish act. I'm glad they're coming out of this war capable of committing such a foolish act. If the reverse had been true, if it had been the S.S. who had taken them prisoner, they would have been lined up and shot, with a song on their lips. I know that I was right, that the S.S. man should have been shot, but I don't regret having kept my mouth shut. I'm pleased that these two young partisans who have knowingly opted for the possibility of dying, who, when they were only seventeen, so often faced death in a war that showed them no quarter, can emerge from this war clean and pure of heart.

Then we look at the trees and the road, and now we're not singing. That is, they aren't singing any more. Night is falling by the time we reach Eisenach.

"Hello there," says the dark-haired girl with the blue eyes.

She came over and sat down beside me on the couch, in the main lounge with the crystal chandeliers.

"What are you doing here?" she says.

"I'm not quite sure any more."

"Are you leaving in the convoy tomorrow?" she asks.

"That must be it," I reply.

There were white tablecloths and glasses of several colors.

There were silver knives, silver spoons, silver forks. There was Moselle wine.

"He was wrong."

"What?" the young woman says.

"Moselle wine is first rate," I say.

"Who are you talking about?" she asks.

"A guy who's dead. A guy from Semur."

She looks at me solemnly. A look I know by heart.

"Semur-en-Auxois?" she says.

"Where else?" And I shrug my shoulders, it's so obvious.

"My parents have a place not far from there," she says.

"With tall trees, a long pathway between, and dead leaves," I tell her.

"How did you know?" she asks.

"Tall trees suit you to a tee," I say.

She shakes her head and stares into space.

"There can't be any dead leaves at this time of year," she says softly.

"There are always dead leaves somewhere," I insist. It must be the Moselle wine.

"Introduce us to this lovely number," Yves says.

We're seated around a low table. There's a bottle of French cognac on the low table. It must be the Moselle wine and the French cognac, but the boys are busy sifting through their memories of the camp. I'm fed up, I can begin to see them sprouting the souls of veterans. I don't want to become a veteran. I'm not a veteran. I'm something else, I'm a veteran of the future. This sudden thought fills me with joy, and the main lounge of the hotel with its crystal chandeliers becomes less absurd. It's a place through which, quite by chance, a veteran of the future is passing.

I gesture vaguely in the direction of the girl with the brown hair and light eyes, and I say: "There she is."

She looks at me, she looks at Yves and the others and says:

"Martine Dupuy."

"There," I say, highly pleased. It must be the Moselle wine, or else the comforting assurance of not being a veteran.

"Mademoiselle Dupuy, may I present a group of veterans."

The boys act as they always do in such cases, taking it as a big joke.

Martine Dupuy turns toward me.

"What about you?" she says in an almost muted voice.

"Not me. I'll never be a veteran."

"Why not?" she says.

"It's a decision I've just made."

She takes out a pack of American cigarettes and offers them all around. Some of them take one. I take one too. She lights her own cigarette, then lights mine.

The boys have already forgotten she's there, and Arnault is explaining to the others, who are shaking their heads, what we were fighting for, we who are now veterans.

"What do you do?" the girl with the blue eyes wants to know. I mean, Martine Dupuy.

I look at her and reply with utter seriousness, as if it were very important. It must be the Moselle wine.

"I hate Charles Morgan, I loathe Valéry, and I've never read *Gone with the Wind*."

Her eyes flutter, and she asks:

"Even *Sparkenbroke*?"

"Especially *Sparkenbroke*," I tell her.

"Why?" she says.

"It took place before the rue Blainville," I explain.

And to me the explanation seems brilliant.

"What's the rue Blainville?" she asks.

"It's a street."

"Of course it's a street, it runs into Contrescarpe Square. What about it?"

"That's where I started to become a man," I tell her.

She looks at me with a bemused smile.

"How old are you?" she says.

"Twenty-one," I reply. "But it's not contagious."

She looks me straight in the eyes and her lips twist into a scornful pout.

"That," she says, "is the kind of remark a veteran would make."

She's right. One should never underestimate people, as I have good reason to know.

"Let's forget that one," I say, a trifle ashamed.

"I'm all for it," she says, and we both laugh.

"Here's to your love life," Arnault says with great solemnity, raising his glass of cognac.

We pour ourselves some French cognac and also drink.

"To your health, Arnault," I say. "You too have participated in the Dada movement."

Arnault stares at me fixedly and, still very solemn, drinks his cognac. The girl with the brown hair and the blue eyes hasn't understood either, and this pleases me no end. Actually, she's nothing but a girl from the smartest section of Paris. I'm delighted about it. Her blue-eyed gaze is like the most legendary of dreams, but the frontiers of her soul are bounded by the Avenue de Neuilly to the north, the Trocadéro to the south, the Avenue Kléber to the east, and the Muette to the west. I'm delighted at being so clever, it must be the Moselle wine.

"And what about you?" I ask her.

"Me?"

"What do you do?"

She buries her nose in her glass of cognac.

"I live on the rue Scheffer," she says softly.

I laugh, this time all by myself.

"That's exactly what I was thinking."

Her blue eyes are amazed by my withering air. I'm becoming aggressive, but it's not the Moselle wine. I want this girl, it's no more complicated than that. We're drinking in silence, and the boys are busy reminding each other how hungry we used to be. But were we really hungry? This evening's dinner was in itself enough to eradicate two years of terrible hunger. I now find it impossible even to conceive of that obsessive hunger. One real meal and hunger has become something abstract. It's nothing more than a notion, an abstract idea. And yet thousands of men died all around me because of that abstract idea. I'm pleased with my body, I find it's a fabulous machine. A single dinner was enough to erase from it that henceforth useless, henceforth abstract thing, that hunger from which we might have died.

"I won't go to see you at the rue Scheffer," I tell the girl.

"You don't like that part of Paris?" she asks.

"It's not that. I mean, I don't know. But it's too far."

"Where do you want to meet, then?" she says.

I look at her blue eyes.

"On the Boulevard Montparnasse, there used to be a place called *Patrick's*."

"Do I remind you of someone," she asks in a low voice.

"Maybe," I tell her, "your blue eyes."

I seem to take it for granted that she's understood that, I mean her looking like someone I used to know. That night, in that charming, old-fashioned hotel at Eisenach, I seem to take it quite for granted.

"Come to see me at Semur," she says. "There are some tall trees, a long pathway between the trees, and maybe even some dead leaves, if we're lucky."

"I doubt it," I tell her, "I doubt that I'll go."

"This night, Jesus! this night will never end," the guy from Semur used to say.

I take a long swig of French cognac, and it was the fourth night of this voyage toward the camp in Germany not far from Weimar. Suddenly I hear music, a tune I know

very well, and I've lost all sense of time or place. What is
In the Shade of the Old Appletree doing here?

"I used to enjoy dancing, when I was younger," I tell
the dark-haired girl.

Our eyes meet, and we burst out laughing.

"I'm sorry," I tell her.

"That's the second time you've started slipping down
veterans' slope," she says.

The French officers have found some records and a record player. They're dancing with the German and French
and Polish girls. The English haven't budged, they couldn't
care less. The Americans are beside themselves with joy,
singing lustily. I glance at the German headwaiters. It
looks as though they are adapting very nicely to their new
life.

"Come on and dance," says the dark-haired girl.

Her body is soft and lithe, and the chandeliers are turning above our heads. We remain in each other's arms while
they put on another record. The music is slower this time,
and the presence of this blue-eyed girl is becoming increasingly clearer.

"How about it, Martine?" says a voice nearby, midway
through the dance.

It's a French officer in combat dress, with a commando
beret on his skull. He looks as though he owns her, and this
girl from the rue Scheffer stops dancing. I suppose there's
nothing left for me to do but rejoin the boys and drink
French cognac.

"Good evening, old pal," the officer says, taking Martine
by the arm.

"Good evening, young man," I answer with great dignity.

His left eyebrow slants upward, but that is his only
visible reaction.

"You just come from the camp?" he says.

"As you can see," I answer.

"It was rough, eh?" the officer with the commando's beret says intently.

"No, not really," I tell him, "it was a ball."

He shrugs his shoulders and leads Martine away.

The boys were still there. They were drinking cognac and telling each other what they were going to do when they got home.

Later, in the room I was sharing with Yves, Yves said to me:

"Why did you let her get away? You looked as though you had it made."

"I don't know. There was some big fucking officer with a beret full of ribbons who came and took charge of her. She looked as though she belonged to him."

"Tough," he says laconically.

Later, still later, after I had recited out loud, without realizing it, the beginning of this old poem: "Arid girl without a smile / Oh solitude and your gray eyes . . ." he grumbled: "If you want to recite poetry, go out into the hall. We have to get up early tomorrow."

I didn't go out into the hall, and we got up at dawn. The city of Eisenach was deserted when the three-truck convoy headed for Paris.

"This night, Jesus! this night will never end," the guy from Semur used to say, and this other night will never end either, this night at Eisenach, in this German hotel room at Eisenach. Was it the strange feeling of being in a real bed, with white sheets and a light, warm eiderdown? Or was it the Moselle wine? Maybe the memory of that girl, the solitude of her gray eyes. The night refused to end, Yves was sleeping the sleep of the just, the night refused to end like the childhood nights of listening for the noise of the elevator announcing that my parents had come home, of listening to the conversations in the garden when Swann came to dinner. I laughed softly to myself, with a joyful lucidity, as I discovered the commonplaces, the abstract, literary snares of my insomnia peopled with dreams. I couldn't sleep. Tomorrow life would begin again, and I didn't know a thing about life. That is, about that life which was going to begin again. I had emerged from the war of my childhood to enter the war of my adolescence, with a slight pause in the middle of a mountain of books. I was completely at ease with any book, with any theory. But in restaurants waiters never saw me signal to them; in department stores I must have become invisible, the clerks never knew I was there. And telephones never did as I bid them, I was forever getting wrong numbers. Girls either had this blue-eyed, inaccessible expression, or else they were so easy it was something mechanical, of no real interest. Tomorrow, life was going to begin again, and I didn't know a thing about that life. I tossed and turned in my bed, vaguely worried. The night would never end, the elevator wasn't stopping at our floor, and I listened for the departure of Swann, who was lingering in the garden, talking. I was tossing and turning in my bed, in that German hotel room at Eisenach, and I was hunting for something comforting in my memory. It was then that I remembered that Jewish woman on the rue de Vaugirard.

In front of the Luxembourg Palace, a truck was unloading stacks of meat for the Wehrmacht cooks. I had glanced at the spectacle, slightly sickened, and continued on my way. I was walking aimlessly, simply because it was too cold in my room. I had two cigarettes left, and I had gone out to get a little warmer by walking and smoking. I had gone past the iron fence of the Luxembourg when I noticed the way that woman looked. As people approached and passed her, she would turn and look after them. One would have thought—that is, I thought—that she was looking for an urgent answer to some vital question in the eyes of the passers-by. She looked the passers-by up and down, as though assessing them: were they worthy of hearing her secret? But she said nothing, she averted her gaze and continued her harassed walking. Why "harassed"? I've asked myself why this ready-made expression "harassed walking" came to mind. I looked at that solitary woman on the sidewalk of the rue de Vaugirard, a few yards in front of me between the rue Jean-Bart and the rue d'Assas. The ready-made expression that had spontaneously come to mind was well taken. A certain curvature of her back, that stiffness of her legs, that slightly stooped left shoulder, all constituted a "harassed walk." I had sized her up properly. Then I said to myself that I was going to cross this woman's path, that she was going to turn and look after me, and that she would have to speak to me. She would, quite simply, have to ask me the question which was plaguing her. For the question was plaguing her, I had seen the expression on her face when she turned to look after the passers-by. I slowed down, so as to delay the moment when I would come abreast of her. For she could have let me pass by, as she had previously let all the others pass by, and that would have been a catastrophe. If she let me pass by, I became someone unworthy of a harassed woman's trust, that woman who was stumbling at practically every step along that interminable rue de Vaugirard. It would really be a low blow if she were to let me pass by, if she were to say nothing to me either.

I came abreast of her. She turned toward me, she looked me up and down. She must have been about thirty. Her face was haggard and wan from that harassing walk, which she had taken not only with her legs, but with her whole being. But her expression was implacable.

"Excuse me," she said, "the Montparnasse Station, do you know where the Montparnasse Station is?"

She had a Slavic accent, what people call a Slavic accent, with a slightly lilting intonation.

I must say I expected something else. I had seen her shy away from at least half a dozen passers-by, at the last minute not daring to ask them the question she had to ask. I was expecting another, altogether more serious question. But I look at her and see from her eyes, which are fixed upon me, from the implacable light in her eyes, that this is the most serious question she has to ask. The Montparnasse Station is really a matter of life or death.

"Yes," I reply, "it's very easy."

And I stop to explain it to her.

She's standing stock still on the sidewalk of the rue de Vaugirard. She breaks into a brief, mournful smile when I tell her that the Montparnasse Station is easy to get to. I don't yet know why she smiled this way, I don't under- stand. I explain the way to her, she listens attentively. I don't yet know she's Jewish, she'll tell me that later while we're walking toward the rue de Rennes. I'll understand why she had that brief, mournful smile. The reason is that near the Montparnasse Station is a friend's house where she may be able to catch her breath after this long, harassing walk. I finally accompany her to that friend's house near the Montparnasse Station.

"Thank you," she says, in front of the house.

"You're sure this is where it is?" I ask her.

She glances at the number above the door.

"Yes," she says. "Thank you for what you've done."

I must have smiled. I think that at that point I must have smiled.

"It wasn't all that tough, you know."

"Tough?"

Her eyebrows arch quizzically.

"I mean, it wasn't all that complicated."

"No," she says.

She looks at the street and at the passers-by. I look at the street and the passers-by with her.

"You would have found it by yourself."

She shakes her head.

"Maybe not," she says. "I was scared to death. As if my heart were dead. Maybe I wouldn't have found it by myself."

I have one cigarette left, I feel like saving it for later.

"You were scared to death?" I asked her.

"Yes," she says. "Paralyzed, frightened to death. I felt all dead inside."

"Well, here you are where you wanted to go," I tell her.

We look at the street, at the passers-by, we smile.

"Anyway, it's not the same thing," she says softly.

"What isn't?" I ask her.

"To find something by yourself or to have someone help you," she says, and she stares far beyond me, into her past.

I feel like asking her why, of all the people passing by, she spoke to me, but I won't do it, actually that's her own business.

She brings her gaze back to me, to the street, to the passers-by.

"You looked as though you were hoping I would speak to you," she says.

We look at each other, I have a feeling we have nothing further to say to each other, or else it will become too involved. She offers me her hand.

"Thank you," she says.

"I'm the one who should thank you," I tell her.

She looks intrigued, the space of a second, then she turns and disappears through the archway of the building.

"Pal, hey pal," says the guy from Semur, "are you asleep?"

Actually, I must have been half-asleep, I have the feeling I was dreaming. Or else dreams are forming around me by themselves, and it's the reality of this boxcar I think I'm dreaming.

"No, I'm not asleep."

"You think this night will soon be over?" asks the guy from Semur.

"I don't know, I haven't the slightest idea."

"I've really had it," he says.

His voice clearly shows it.

"Try to get a little sleep."

"Oh no, that's worse," says the guy from Semur.

"Why?"

"I dream that I'm falling, I can't stop falling."

"Me too."

It's true that you fall, irremediably. You fall into a well, from the top of a cliff, you fall into the water. But that night I was happy to fall into the water, to slip down into the rustling silk of the water, with my mouth full, my lungs full. It was the endless water, the fathomless water, the great maternal water. I awoke with a start when my body bent and slumped over, and it was worse. The boxcar and the night in the boxcar were much worse than the nightmare.

"I don't think I'm going to make it," says the guy from Semur.

"You make me laugh," I tell him.

"Really, pal, I feel all dead inside."

That reminds me of something.

"What do you mean, dead?" I ask him.

"I mean dead, not alive."

"Your heart too?" I ask him.

"Yes, my heart too," he says.

Someone behind us begins to scream. The voice rises, and then fades into a muted moan and then starts in again, louder than ever.

"If he doesn't stop we're going to crack up," says the guy from Semur.

I feel he's completely tense, I can hear his breath coming in short gasps.

"Crack up, yeah, that'll serve you right," says the voice behind us.

The guy from Semur turns part way around toward the dark mass of bodies stacked behind us.

"That bastard still hasn't kicked off," he says.

The guy mutters a few vulgarities.

"Be polite," says the guy from Semur, "and let us talk in peace."

The guy laughs sardonically.

"You're great ones for talking, you guys," he says.

"We enjoy it," I say. "Remember, getting there is half the fun."

"If you don't like it," adds the guy from Semur, "you can get out at the next stop."

The guy laughs.

"We're all getting out at the next stop."

For once he's right.

"Don't worry," says the guy from Semur, "wherever we go we'll be watching you."

"Sure," says another voice off to the left, "we always keep a close watch on informers."

With that, the guy shuts up.

The scream of a while back has softened to a whispered, interminable, overwhelming moan.

"What does it mean," I ask the guy from Semur, "to feel as though your heart's dead."

It was a year ago, more or less, on the rue de Vaugirard. She had said to me: "My heart feels dead, I feel all dead inside." I wonder if her heart has started to live again. She didn't know whether or not she would be able to stay very long with her friend. Perhaps she was forced to begin walking again. I wonder whether she hasn't already taken this voyage that the guy from Semur and I are taking.

"I wouldn't know how to tell you," says the guy from Semur. "You don't feel anything in your heart, like a hole, or else like a very heavy stone."

I wonder whether, finally, she took this voyage that we're taking. In any case, I still don't know that, if indeed she has taken this voyage, she hasn't taken it the same way we are. Because there's still another way of traveling, for the Jews, I was to see that later. I have only a vague picture of this voyage that she has perhaps taken, because I still don't have a clear picture of the kind of voyage they make the Jews take. Later on I'll have a clear picture.

Nor do I know that I'll see this woman again, after these voyages are gone and forgotten. She was in the garden of the house at Saint-Prix, years after my return from this voyage, and I found it perfectly natural to come upon her suddenly in the chilly sun of early spring. At the entrance to the village, where the road begins to ascend toward the *Lapin Sauté* restaurant, they had divided into lots the big park which used to descend gently toward Saint-Leu. I had just walked through the forest at dawn, with all the weight of a wasted, sleepless night on my shoulders. I had left the others behind in the big room where the same jazz records were playing over and over, and I had taken a long walk in the forest before descending again toward Saint-Prix. On the square, the façade of the house had recently been restored. The door was half open, and I pushed it. To the right, the corridor leads to the garden, and I crossed the lawn, shivering in the spring sun, after my sleepless night. In the forest, while I had been taking the long walk in the forest, I had felt an urge to hear the sound of the bell on the garden gate again. I opened and closed the garden gate several times, to hear the rusty, metallic sound I remembered, the sound of the little bell activated by the gate. It was then I turned around and saw a woman watching me. She was stretched out on a lounge chair, near the shed where the firewood used to be kept. "Do you hear that?" I say to her. "What?" says the woman. "The sound," I say, "the sound of the bell." "Yes," she says. "I like it," I say. The woman looks at me while I cross the lawn and come over to her. "I'm a friend of Madame Wolff," she says, and I find it quite natural that she's there and that she's a friend of Madame Wolff and that, once again, spring is in the air. I ask her if the house still belongs to Madame Wolff, and she looks at me. "You haven't been here for a long time?" she says. I suppose it's been five or six years since my family left this house. "About six years," I tell her. "Do you like the sound of the garden bell?" she says. I tell her that I still like it. "I do too," she says, but I have the feeling she would rather be alone. "Did you just happen to come in here?" she asks me, and I have the feeling that she'd be pleased if I had just happened to come in, that I hadn't come for any specific reason. "Not at all," I tell her, and I explain that I wanted to see the garden again and also hear the sound the garden bell made. "Actually, I came a good distance, just for that." "Do you know Madame Wolff?" she says hurriedly, as if she wanted at all cost to avoid my telling her what really brought me here. "Of course I do," I tell her. There's a folding chair beside the lawn chair, with a closed book and a half-filled glass of water on it. I move the book and the glass of water and sit down. "You don't smoke?" I say. She shakes her head, and I wonder whether she isn't going to run away. I light a cigarette and ask her why she likes the sound of the bell. She shrugs her shoulders. "Because it's like something from out of the past," she says dryly. "I see," I say, and smile. But she sits up in the lounge chair and leans forward. "You wouldn't understand," she says. I look at her. "Yes I would," I say, "it's a memory for me too." I lean over toward her and take her right arm, her wrist, and my fingers lightly graze her white, delicate skin and the blue number from Oswiecim tattooed on her white, delicate, already slightly withered skin. "I was wondering," I tell her, "I was wondering whether you had finally made this voyage." Then she withdraws her arm, which she hugs to her breast, and she retreats as far as possible into the lounge chair. "Who are you?" she says. Her voice is choked. "In the Moselle valley," I tell her, "I wondered whether you had made this voyage." She looks at me, breathing heavily. "Later on, too, when I saw the trainloads of Jews evacuated from Poland, I wondered whether you had made this voyage." Silently she begins to cry. "But who are you?" she begs. I shake my head. "I wondered whether that house on the rue Bourdelle, behind the Montparnasse Station, was going to be a lasting shelter, or whether it would only be a way-station before you began your journey again." "I don't know you," she says. I tell her that I recognized her immediately, that is, I realized immediately that I knew her, even before I recognized her. She's still crying silently. "I don't know who you are," she says. "Leave me alone." "You don't know who I am, but once you recognized me," I tell her. I remember the look on her face, a look out of the past on the rue de Vaugirard, but now she no longer has that same implacable expression. "The rue de Vaugirard," I say, "in '41 or '42, I can't remember which." She buries her head in her hands. "You wanted to know how to get to the Montparnasse Station, you didn't dare ask anyone passing by. But you asked me." " I don't remember," she says. "You were hunting for the rue Antoine-Bourdelle, actually. I took you there." "I don't remember," she says. "You were going to some friends' house on the rue Antoine-Bourdelle, don't you remember?" I say. "I remember that street and that house, yes, I remember," she says. "You had on a blue overcoat," I tell her. "I don't remember," she says. But I persist, I'm still clinging to the hope that she'll remember. "You were lost," I tell her, "you didn't know how to find the Montparnasse Station. I was the one who helped you." Then she looks at me and almost shouts: "No one has *ever* helped me." I can feel that it's over, that I ought to leave. "I was helped all the time," I tell her. "No one," she says, "ever." I look at her, and I can see that she's quite sincere, that she's thoroughly convinced of what she's saying. "Maybe I was lucky," I say, "all my life I've run into people who have helped me." Then she shouts again: "You're not a Jew, that's all." I snuff out my cigarette on the grass. "It's true," I tell her, "I've never been a Jew. There were times when I've regretted it." Now I'm under the impression that she'd like to insult me, by her derisive laugh, her impenetrable expression, by the open wound on her stony face. "You don't know what you're saying," she says. "I don't know," I say, "I know that Hans is dead." Then there was a silence, and I have to leave. "Are you sure you saw me on the rue de Vaugirard in '42?" she says. My hand makes a vague gesture. "If you've forgotten, it's as though I didn't see you." "What?" she says. "If you've forgotten, then it's true that I didn't see you. It's true that we don't know each other." Having said that, I get up. "It's a misunderstanding," I tell her. "Please forgive me." "I don't remember," she says. "I'm sorry." "It's not important," I tell her, and I leave.

But I don't yet know that she's made this voyage and that she's returned from it dead, immured in her solitude.

"You know what time it is?" a voice behind us says.

No one answers, since no one has any idea what time it is. It's just plain night. The night whose end is not in sight. Moreover, right now the night has no end, it is really eternal, ensconced forever in its endless "nightness." Even if we had been able to keep our watches, even if the S.S. hadn't confiscated all our watches, even if we had been able to see what time it was, I wonder if knowing the time would have had any concrete significance. Perhaps it would only have been an abstract reference to the outside world where time really passes, where it has its own density, its duration. But for us, in the boxcar, the night is really only a muted shadow, night detached from everything that is not night.

"We're not moving, we haven't been moving for hours," a voice behind us says.

"Maybe you thought we had top priority?" someone says.

I seem to recognize that last voice. I think it belongs to the guy who said he was a real clown at the time of that pisscan incident. Yes, I'm sure it's his. I can begin to distinguish the voices on this voyage.

Later, in a few months, I'll know what kind of voyages they made the Jews take. When the Russians began their all-out winter offensive in Poland, I'd see the trains arriving at the camp station. They were evacuating the Jews from the Polish camps, the Jews they hadn't had time to exterminate, or maybe they figured they could still squeeze a little work out of them. The winter of the following year had been a hard winter. I saw the trainloads of Jews arrive, the transports of Jews evacuated from the Polish camps. There were almost two hundred padlocked in each boxcar, some eighty more than we had had in ours. That night, next to the guy from Semur, I hadn't tried to picture what it could be like to be two hundred in a boxcar like ours. Later, yes, when I saw the trainloads of Jews from Poland, I did try to picture it. And that winter of the following year had been a harsh one. The Jews from Poland have traveled six, eight, ten days, in the cold of that harsh winter. With nothing to eat, of course, and nothing to drink. When they arrived, when they pulled back the sliding doors, nobody moved. They had to pry loose the frozen mass of corpses, the Polish Jews dead standing up, frozen standing up— they fell like tenpins onto the station platform of the camp —in order to find the few survivors. For there were some survivors. A slow, stumbling band began to walk toward the camp entrance. Some fell, never again to rise, others got up, and still others literally dragged themselves. One day, in the agglutinant mass of corpses in one boxcar, we found three Jewish kids. The oldest was five. The German pals of the "Lagerschutz" sneaked them out under the noses of the S.S. These three Jewish orphans we had found in the congealed mass of corpses lived in the camp and got out alive. This was how I learned, during that harsh winter, how they made the Jews travel.

But this year, beside my pal from Semur who was suddenly sick at heart, who felt dead inside, it occurred to me that maybe that Jewish woman from the rue de Vaugirard had already made this voyage. Maybe she too had gazed out at the Moselle valley with her implacable eyes.

Outside, we hear the sound of orders being barked, of hurried footsteps, of boots on the embankment beside the tracks.

"We're leaving," I say.

"You think so?" asks the guy from Semur.

"It sounds as though they're calling back the guards."

We stand stock still in the dark, waiting.

The train blows its whistles and, with a jerk, begins to move.

"Oh look, pal, look!" says the guy from Semur excitedly.

I look, and dawn is breaking. It's a grayish fringe on the horizon, growing larger. Dawn, another night gone, one less night of this voyage. It's true that this night was endless, it had no foreseeable end. Dawn bursts within us, it's still only a narrow gray line on the horizon, but now nothing can stop it from spreading. Dawn unfolds by itself, out of its own night, unfolds toward itself, toward its glowing annihilation.

"That's it, pal, that's it," sings the guy from Semur.

In the boxcar, everyone begins talking at once, and the train rolls on.

I made the return trip in the trees. That is, my eyes were full of trees, full of the leaves of trees, full of green branches. I was stretched out in the back of the truck, which was covered with a tarpaulin, I was looking up at the sky and the sky was full of trees. It's amazing how many trees there are between Eisenach and Longuyon, in the spring sky. Also, from time to time, airplanes. It's true the war wasn't over, but these ridiculous planes seemed unreal, out of place in the spring sky. I had eyes only for the trees, for the green branches of the trees. It's really restful to travel that way.

Toward evening on the second day of the trip, I was dozing with my eyes open, when suddenly my ears were struck by an explosion of voices.

"This is it boys, this is it!"

Some character with a shrill voice has begun singing the *Marseillaise*. It was the Colonel, no doubt, he was the only one capable of doing such a thing.

I was comfortable, I had no desire to move. All that activity was too much for me.

"This is it, boys, we're home, boys, home!"

"Have you seen it, men? This is France!"

"We're in France, boys, this is France!"

"Long live France!" cried the Colonel's shrill voice, which of course interrupted the rendition of the *Marseillaise*. But the *Marseillaise* began all over again, you could count on the Colonel.

I looked up at the trees, and the trees hadn't given me any warning. If I were to believe these shouts, a while back the trees were German and here the trees are French, according to my traveling companions. I looked at the leaves on the trees. They were the same green as before. Obviously my eyes must not be very good. If someone had asked the Colonel, he would surely have seen the difference. He would never have mistaken a French tree for a German tree.

Someone's shaking me by the shoulder.

"Hey there, pal, where have you been?" he says. "We're home."

"I'm not," I tell him, without budging.

"What do you mean?" the guy asks.

I half sit up and look at him. He looks suspicious.

"I'm not home. I'm not French."

His face lights up.

"Of course," he says, "I forgot. With you one tends to forget. You talk exactly like us."

I don't feel like explaining to him why I talk exactly as they do, why I talk like the Colonel, without any accent, that is, with a real French accent. This is the surest way of preserving my status as a foreigner, which I cherish above all. If I had an accent, my "foreignness" would be constantly apparent. It would become something banal, exteriorized. Personally, I would get used to the banality of being taken for a foreigner. Similarly, being a foreigner would then no longer be any problem, it would no longer have any meaning. That's why I don't have any accent, why, from the language point of view, I eliminated any possibility of being taken for a foreigner. In a certain sense, being a foreigner has become an internal virtue.

"That doesn't matter," the guy says. "We're not going to quibble over such trifles on a day like this. Anyway, France is your adopted country."

The guy is pleased, he gives me a friendly smile.

"Thanks a lot," I tell him, "one country is plenty. I can't see myself dragging a second one around on my back."

The guy's put out. He has offered me the most precious

gift he was capable of giving, or that he thought he was capable of giving. He has made me a Frenchman-by-adoption. In a sense, he's authorizing me to be like himself, and I refuse the gift.

He's put out and leaves me.

Sometime I'll have to give some serious thought to that habit so many French people have of thinking that France is everyone's second country. I'll have to try and find out why it is so many French people are so smug about being French, so rationally satisfied to be French.

For the moment, I don't feel like pondering such problems. I go on looking up at the trees parading past above me, between me and the sky. I look at the green leaves; the leaves are French. The boys are back home, more power to them.

I remember one winter a few years ago, I was waiting in a big room of the Central Police Station. I was there to have my temporary resident's permit renewed, and the big room was filled with other foreigners who, like me, were there for the same, or for a similar, reason.

I was in a waiting line, it was a long waiting line that started at a table over at the far end of the room. At the table was a little man whose cigarette was constantly going out. And he was constantly relighting his cigarette. The little man examined everyone's papers, or the summonses they were carrying, in order to direct them to this or that window. Sometimes he simply shouted and sent them packing. The dowdy little man wanted to make sure no one had the least doubt, that no one mistook him for what he seemed to be, a dowdy little man whose cigarette was constantly going out. So he sometimes shouted, he insulted the people, especially the women. Who did we think we were, who did all we damn aliens think we were? The little man was the incarnation of power, he never missed a trick, he was a pillar of the new order. Who did we think we were, showing up a day later than the date marked on the summons? The people offered their explanations. Work, a sick wife, children to take care of. But the little man wasn't to be taken in by these ludicrous explanations, by this obvious insincerity. He was going to show us what he was made of, you bastards are going to see what I'm made of, he was going to show us that we should make no mistake about him, that he had you-know-what-you-know-where. He was going to put these damn foreigners in their places, all right. And then suddenly he forgot that he was the terrifying incarnation of power, and for several long minutes he sucked on his cigarette butt without saying a word. Silence settled over the big room, over the welter of whispers and the sound of shoes scraping the floor.

I was fascinated by the spectacle of the little man. I didn't even find that time was dragging. Finally my turn came and I found myself in front of the little table, the little man, and his cigarette butt which, in fact, had just gone out again. He takes the receipt for my temporary resident's permit and shakes it with an air of disgust, at the same time giving me a withering look. I don't flinch, I stare at him intently, this guy fascinates me.

He lays the receipt on the table, relights his butt, and looks at the receipt.

"Ah ha," he says in a loud voice, "a Spanish Red."

He seems overjoyed. It must be a long time since he's had a Spanish Red to pick on.

I vaguely remember the port of Bayonne in southern France, the arrival of the trawler in the port of Bayonne. The boat had tied up next to the main square, there were big beds of flowers, and summer vacationers. We gazed at these scenes from out of an earlier life. It was at Bayonne that I first heard us referred to as Spanish Reds.

I look at the little man, I say nothing, I'm thinking vaguely about that day years before at Bayonne. Anyway, there's never anything you can say to a cop.

"How about that," he shouts, "a Spanish Red!"

He looks at me, I look at him. I know that everyone is watching us. So I stand up a little straighter. I have a tendency to be slightly stooped. It was in vain that they told me to stand up straight, nothing doing, I always stand with my shoulders slightly hunched. I can't help it, I feel more at ease with myself that way. But now I stand as straight as I can. I don't want them to take my natural posture for an attitude of submissiveness. The thought horrifies me.

I look at the little man, he looks at me. Suddenly he explodes.

"I'll teach you, you bastards, me, yes, me. I'll goddamn well teach you to screw around with me. And for a start, you can go back to the end of the line and begin all over again."

I don't reply. I retrieve my piece of paper from the table and turn my back on him. His butt has gone out again, and this time he snuffs it out furiously in the ash tray.

I walk back across the room, all the way back along the waiting line, thinking about that strange habit cops have of always using the familiar form of address. Maybe they think it impresses us. But that sad son of a bitch doesn't know what he's done. He called me a Spanish Red, and now, suddenly, I'm no longer alone in the big gray, innocuous room. From one end of the waiting line to the other I saw the expressions open and flower, saw the birth, in all that gray, of the most beautiful smiles in the world. I'm still holding my paper in my hand, for two cents I'd tear it up and toss the pieces into the air. I resume my place at the end of the line. The guys move in around me and smile. They were alone, I was alone, and now we're all together. The little man has won.

I'm lying in the truck, looking up at the trees. It was at Bayonne, on the docks next to the main square of Bayonne, that I learned I was a Spanish Red. The next day I got my

second surprise, when we read in a newspaper that there
were Reds and Nationalists. Why they were Nationalists
when they fought the war using Moroccan troops, the
Foreign Legion, German planes and the Littorio divisions,
was more than I could fathom. That was one of the initial
mysteries of the French language I had to decipher. But
at Bayonne, on the docks at Bayonne, I became a Spanish
Red. There were big beds of flowers, and lots of summer
vacationers behind the *gendarmes* who had come to see
the Spanish Reds disembark. We were vaccinated, and
they let us disembark. The summer vacationers looked at
the Spanish Reds, and we looked at the shopwindows of
the bakeries. We looked at the white bread, the golden
croissants, all these things from out of the past. We were
like fish out of water in this world from out of the past.

Since then I've never stopped being a Spanish Red. It's
a way of life that was valid everywhere. Thus, in the camp
I was a *Rotspanier.* I looked at the trees and I was happy
to be a Spanish Red. The years were going by, I was more
and more pleased to go by that name.

Suddenly there were no more trees, and the truck
stopped. We're at Longuyon, the repatriation camp. We jump
down out of the truck, and my legs are asleep. Some nurses
come over, and the Colonel kisses them all. The joy of
being home, no doubt. After that it's a real circus. We
have to drink some broth and answer a lot of asinine
questions.

As I listened to these questions I suddenly made a decision. I have to admit that this decision had already been
maturing within me. I had vaguely thought about it in the
trees between Eisenach and here. I believe it was already
in the process of maturing from the time I first saw the
boys turning into veterans in the lounge at the Eisenach
hotel, beneath the chandeliers of the Eisenach hotel. Perhaps it even began to mature earlier. Perhaps, even before

I returned from this voyage, I had been in a frame of mind to make this decision. In any case, as I mechanically answered these asinine questions—were you very hungry? were you cold? were you terribly miserable?—I decided never again to talk about this voyage, never again to allow myself to be placed in the position of having to answer questions about this voyage. I knew, though, that this would not be possible, never to talk about it. But at least a long period of silence, years of silence about this voyage, God, that was the only way to survive it. Maybe later, when no one talked about it any more, maybe then I would talk about it. That possibility floated dimly on the horizon of my decision.

We had been dragged from pillar to post, and we finally ended up in a room where they had taken us for a physical examination.

When it was my turn, I had a chest X-ray taken, a cardiogram, and was examined by the dentist. They weighed me, checked my height and asked me a lot of questions about any childhood sicknesses I had had. At the end of the line, I found myself seated before a doctor who had a complete file on me, compiled by the various specialists.

"This is extraordinary," the doctor says, after checking my file.

I look at him, and he offers me a cigarette.

"This is incredible," the doctor says. "It seems there's nothing seriously the matter with you."

I make some vaguely interested gesture, because I'm not exactly sure what he's talking about.

"Nothing wrong with the lungs, heart all right, blood pressure normal. It's incredible," the doctor repeats.

I smoke the cigarette he has offered me and try to realize that it's incredible, I try to picture myself as an incredible case. I feel like telling this doctor that it's being alive which is incredible, of being in the skin of someone alive. Even if my blood pressure were abnormal, it would still be incredible to be alive.

"You do have a couple of teeth that need filling," the doctor says. "But that of course is to be expected."

"That's the least that could be expected," I say, so as not to let him do all the talking.

"For weeks I've been seeing deportees coming through here," he tells me, "and yours is the first case where everything seems to be completely in order."

He looks at me for a moment and adds:

"Or so it seems."

"Oh?" I say politely.

He looks at me attentively, as though he's afraid he might suddenly spot the signs of some unknown illness which had escaped the observation of the specialists.

"Do you want me to tell you?" he asks.

Actually I don't, it really doesn't interest me. But he didn't ask me that question to find out whether or not I want him to tell me, he's already made up his mind to tell me anyway.

"I can tell you, since you're in perfect shape," he says.

Then he pauses briefly and adds:

"Or so it seems."

The eternal scientific doubt. This man has learned to be prudent, it's understandable.

"I can tell you," he goes on, "most of the men who have been through here will not survive."

He waxes enthusiastic, he seems enamored of his subject. He launches into a long medical explanation about the foreseeable consequences of deportation. And I begin to feel slightly ashamed of being in such good shape. Or so it seems. It wouldn't take much for me to find myself suspect. It wouldn't take much to make me tell him it's not my fault. It wouldn't take much for me to start apologizing for having survived, of still having a good chance of surviving.

"Let me tell you, most of you are not going to survive. What proportion that will be, only the future will tell. But I don't believe I'm wrong in predicting that sixty percent of the survivors will die during the coming months or years, as a result of their deportation."

I feel like telling him that all this is no longer any concern of mine, that I've crossed it out. I feel like telling him that he annoys the hell out of me, that whether I live or die is no concern of his. In any event, my pal from Semur is dead, I feel like telling him. But the man is doing his job, I can't keep him from doing his job.

He bids me good-bye, and it seems I'm damned lucky. It's almost as though I should be happy I took this voyage. If I hadn't taken this voyage, I would never have known how damned lucky I was. I have to admit that at that moment the world of the living is somewhat disconcerting to me.

Outside, Haroux was waiting for me.

"How about it, pal," he says to me, "you going to be O.K.?"

"To hear the doc talk, I apparently will. In fact I'm in such good shape the place must have been a real sanatorium."

"Not me," Haroux says. "Seems like my heart isn't all it should be. Have to go get a real check-up in Paris."

"The heart's no real problem, you just have to stop using it, that's all."

"You think it bothers me, pal?" Haroux says. "We're here, the sun is shining, we could have gone up in smoke."

"True," I say.

Actually, we should have gone up in smoke. We joke about it together. Haroux joins in too, we have the right to laugh about it if we want to. And the fact is we do want to.

"Come on," Haroux says, "we have to go and get some temporary identity papers."

"Jesus, that's right. It's starting all over again."

We start off in the direction of the administration building.

"Come off it, man," Haroux says, "you don't want them to let you go running around loose without any papers, do you? Just in case you might be somebody else."

"What proof do they have that I'm not sombody else? Here we show up fresh as daisies. We may be somebody else?"

Haroux's enjoying himself.

"And what about swearing on the Bible, pal? We're going to swear on the Bible who we are. You mean you don't take swearing on the Bible seriously?"

Haroux's enjoying himself. He has a heart that's not all it should be, certainly the doctor's including him among the sixty percent who won't survive, but the sun is shining and we could have gone up in smoke.

"You're in rare form, Haroux."

"Rare form? You bet your sweet life. I'm floating on air, pal, that's how I feel."

"You're lucky. I find all these nurses, these asinine questions, these doctors, these pitying expressions, these shaking heads really depressing."

Haroux explodes, he can't stop laughing.

"You take all that too seriously, old man, I've always told you that. Your head's too big. Let yourself go, pal, do what I do, laugh about it. Don't you find all these civilians hilarious?"

We go into the administration building, and he casts a wide glance around at all the civilian lads and lasses.

"Anyway," he says, "we're not yet back in the swing of it, you understand."

That must be it, of course.

With the help of swearing on the Bible, the formalities of identification take relatively little time, all in all. We find ourselves at the end of the row before a blond young woman in a white blouse who takes Haroux's paper and writes something on it. Then she gives Haroux a thousand-franc note and eight packs of *gauloises* cigarettes. Because she's the lady in charge of repatriation bonuses. She takes my paper and my temporary identity card. She writes something on the paper and lines up eight packs of *gauloises* on the table. I begin putting them in my pocket, but there are too many, I have to keep half of them in my hand. Then she hands me the thousand-franc note. Haroux gives me a *gauloise*, and we light them. The blond young woman glances at my identity card just as she was about to return it to me.

"Oh!" she says, "you're not French!"

"No," I tell her.

"You're really not?" she says, looking at my card.

"France is my adopted country, so they tell me, but I'm not really French."

She looks at me, and then she looks more closely at the card.

"What are you?" she asks.

"You can see, I'm a Spanish refugee."

"And you're not a naturalized citizen?" she persists.

"Miss, wait till I'm dead before you stuff me."

After I said it I was slightly ashamed. That was another veteran's joke, as the brunette from Eisenach would say.

"But this is serious, monsieur," she tells me in a bureaucratic tone. "You're really not French?"

"Really not."

Beside me, Haroux is beginning to grow impatient.

"What difference does it make whether my mate is French or Turkish?" he asks.

"I'm not Turkish," I say softly.

Just to keep things straight.

"So he's not French, what the hell difference does it make?" Haroux asks.

The blond woman is taken slightly aback.

"You see," she says, "it's a matter of the repatriation bonus. Only French citizens are entitled to it."

"I'm not a French citizen," I explain to her. "In fact, I'm not a citizen at all."

"You're not going to tell me he isn't entitled to this lousy thousand-franc note," Haroux shouts.

"But that's just it," the blond young woman says, "he isn't entitled to it."

"And who made that lousy goddamned decision?" Haroux shouts.

The blond woman is becoming more and more upset.

"Please control your temper, sir, it's not my fault, it's the Administration."

Haroux bursts into a violent laugh.

"Administration my balls," he says. "And you think that's just dandy?"

"But it's not my job to think, monsieur," she says.

"You have no personal opinion on the matter?" Haroux asks spitefully.

"If I had to have personal opinions, monsieur, there would be no end to it," she says, sincerely shocked. "I confine myself to carrying out the Administration's orders," she adds.

"Your mother..." says Haroux venomously.

"My mother is also a civil servant, monsieur," she says, increasingly annoyed.

"Forget it," I tell Haroux. "You can see she has her orders."

Haroux gives me a withering glance.

"Shut up," he says. "You're not French, this is no concern of yours. For me it's a question of principle."

"The instructions are quite clear, sir. We have them in writing. Only French citizens are entitled to the repatriation bonus," the young woman says.

"So we fought this war for nothing," Haroux says.

"Stop exaggerating."

"Shut up," he says. "It's a question of principle."

"The fact is," I insist, "I didn't fight this war."

"What the Christ are you talking about?" Haroux says, furious.

"Just what I said, I didn't fight it, that's all."

"What the hell does that mean, anyway?" he asks me.

He turned toward me, and the blond young woman is watching us. She's still holding my temporary identity card in her hand.

"It means that I'm not a veteran. It means that I didn't fight this war."

"You're crazy. What did you do then?"

"I was in the Resistance," I tell him.

"Don't split hairs, d'you mind? Don't you think you're entitled to that lousy repatriation bonus?"

"Oh, I'm sorry," the young woman says, annoyed, "that's not the repatriation bonus. It's only an advance. The exact amount of the bonus hasn't been settled yet."

This young woman wants everything to be absolutely clear. That's how they are in the Administration.

"Advance my balls," Haroux says.

"Don't be vulgar," the young woman says.

Haroux explodes again into a violent laugh.

"So, do you or don't you want this goddamned advance?"

"But I haven't been repatriated," I say innocently.

"You're nuts," Haroux says.

"But sir," says the young woman, "it's not a question of

whether monsieur does or does not want it, it's the fact
that he isn't *entitled* to it. Do you understand? It's a question of being *entitled* to it."

"It's a question of shit," says Haroux with finality.

The noise of the discussion has attracted attention to
us. Some guy comes over to us. He's not wearing a white
smock, he has on a blue suit. He must be the section chief
of this Administration which is administering our return to
the world. He inquires politely as to the cause of the discussion. Haroux explains it to him, in strong words and with
a few pointed reflections concerning the state of France.
The blond young woman also explains to him, administratively, in a noncommital tone. It's a matter which con-
cerns her administratively, she doesn't have to take sides.

The section chief in the blue suit politely explains to us
what the Administration's decisions are. It's quite clear that
I have to give back this thousand-franc note. "However,
you should note that monsieur will certainly become entitled to it at some future date when the question of the
repatriation bonus and the status of refugees will have been
clarified legally. The question will necessarily be raised, in
its entirety, because there are many foreigners who have
fought for France, as has monsieur." I don't feel like telling
him that I haven't fought for France and that, in any case,
I haven't been repatriated. I hand back the thousand-franc
note to which I am not entitled. "Moreover, monsieur is
entitled to transportation and free lodging throughout
France until he arrives at his place of residence. The question of his status as a repatriated person can be examined in
its entirety there, at his place of residence." I don't tell
him that I have no place of residence. Perhaps that would
complicate the question of my lodging and free transportation throughout France. Haroux has nothing further to offer.
He seems overwhelmed by all these administrative con-
siderations. We're on the point of leaving.

"And the cigarettes?" asks the blond young woman.

The question of the cigarettes, suddenly raised again, causes the section chief in the blue suit to blink his eyes.

"The cigarettes," he repeats.

Haroux throws up his hands, by now he's speechless.

But the section chief has made a quick, courageous decision.

"To be sure," he says, "according to the letter of that memorandum, the cigarettes and the advance of a thousand francs are linked together. But I believe that we will be adhering to the spirit of that memorandum if we give monsieur the cigarettes. Unless, of course, monsieur doesn't smoke."

"The fact is," I retort, "I smoke a lot."

"Then keep the cigarettes," he says, "keep them. The spirit of the memorandum authorizes you to keep them."

Haroux stares into space, left and right. Perhaps he's trying to spot the spirit of that memorandum.

"Good luck, gentlemen," says the section chief, "and have a good trip home."

The sly little lares and penates on my hearthstone must be having a ball right now. Haroux and I find ourselves back out in the courtyard.

"It's unbelievable," Haroux says.

I don't dare tell him that I find the whole thing fairly significant, he seems too upset. We walk down the main road of the repatriation camp. But the fact is I'm not repatriated, I'm almost grateful to that blond woman for having reminded me. I'm going from one foreign country to another foreign country. That is, I'm the one who's a foreigner. I'm almost pleased to have rediscovered, at one fell swoop, my "foreignness"; it helps me maintain a proper perspective. Haroux, of course, has a different point of view. Haroux is sad to realize how stable is the administrative edifice of his country. On Sunday, at the camp, he probably dreamed, when we had time enough to dream, of a totally new France. This shocking contact with reality saddens him. Haroux doesn't utter another word. As for me, I have always felt that the contacts with reality are prodigiously stimulating to the mind. They make you think, no doubt about it.

We're walking down the main road of the Longuyon camp, and we pause to take a drink at a fountain. Haroux is the first to drink, he wipes his mouth with the back of his hand.

"The whole thing's as stupid as hell," he says.

I find he's exaggerating, that death is much more stupid still. I too take a drink of the cool water. I'm thinking that this voyage is over. The cool water flows down my throat, and I remember that other fountain on the square of that German village. Haroux was there too, in fact. We were walking down the white road, and it was alternately sunny and shady. The buildings of the Little Camp were off to the right, in among the trees. We were going to get a drink. Yesterday, as they fled, the S.S. blew up the water mains. But there must be a fountain on the square of this village. There's certainly a fountain, we're going to get a drink.

Our boots strike the stones and pebbles on the white road, we're talking in loud voices. There must be a fountain on the village square. On Sundays, we sometimes used to look at this village set in the verdant plain. We were in the woods just beyond the barracks of the Little Camp, and we were looking at this village. There was quiet smoke above the houses of this village. But today we're outside, we're walking along this rocky road, we're talking in loud voices. The village must be expecting us, it's at the end of our victorious march, in fact, it *is* the end of our march.

I look at the trees, the trees are moving. The April wind

is in the trees. The landscape has ceased to be motionless. Earlier, under the slow, immutable rhythm of the seasons, the landscape was motionless. That is, we were motionless in a landscape which was merely a setting. But the landscape has begun to stir. Each path which forks off to the left, beneath the trees, is a way leading into the depths of the countryside, toward the perpetual renewal of the countryside. All these potential joys, within arm's reach, make me laugh. Haroux was walking on ahead; he stops and waits for me. He looks at me laughing, all by myself.

"Why are you laughing all by yourself?" he asks.

"It's funny to be walking down a road."

I turn and glance about me. He does too.

"Yes," he says, "it's pretty funny."

We light our cigarettes. They're Camels, an American soldier gave them to me. He was from New Mexico, he spoke a little Spanish.

"Spring," I tell Haroux, "spring and the country have always made me laugh."

"And why is that?" he wants to know.

His hair is white, cut very short, and he's asking me why spring, and the country, always make me laugh.

We turn back and look at the camp.

The barracks of the quarantine camp, the buildings of the "Revier" are partly hidden by the trees. Higher up, on the side of this hill, are the sections made of concrete, standing row on row, and fronting the square where roll call used to be held, the wooden barracks, painted a pretty, springlike green. Off to the left, in the distance, the crematorium chimney. We look at the denuded hill, where men have built a camp. There is silence and the April sky over the camp that men have built.

I try to realize that this is a unique moment, that we have tenaciously survived for this unique moment when we could look at the camp from the outside. But I can't manage it. I can't manage to capture what is unique in this moment. I say to myself: Look, friend, this is a unique moment, there are loads of guys who are dead, they used to dream of this moment, when we would be able to look at the camp like this, from the outside, when we would no longer be inside, but outside—I tell myself all that, but it doesn't excite me. Obviously I have no special talent for capturing unique moments, in all their limpid purity. I see the camp, I can hear the silent murmur of spring, and it makes me feel like laughing, like sprinting down the paths toward the undergrowth, the delicate green undergrowth, the way the country, the spring, always make me feel.

I missed that unique moment.

"Hey, are you coming?" Diego shouts, a hundred yards farther down.

And we hurry along.

We were thirsty, we said to ourselves that there must be a fountain on the village square. There are always fountains on the squares of little country villages. The cool water spills from these fountains, down onto the stones polished by centuries. We quickly overtake Diego and Pierre, who are waiting for us at the crossroads of the macadam road leading to the village.

"What the hell were you doing?" Diego asks.

"Spring makes him laugh. He stops and laughs himself sick," Haroux says.

"Spring fever, that's all," Pierre states flatly.

"No it's not," I say, "not yet anyway. But it's funny to be walking along a road. Till yesterday, it was the others who were out walking along the roads."

"What others?" Diego asks.

"All the others, everybody who wasn't inside."

"There were a lot of us inside," Pierre says.

That's true, there were a lot of us.

"Come on," Diego says, "are we going to this goddamned village?"

Mechanically we glance toward the end of this road, at this goddamned village. Actually, it's not mainly thirst enticing us to this village. We could have drunk the water the Americans brought in their tank-trucks. It's the village itself which attracts us. The village was the outside, the outside where life went on. On Sunday, at the edge of the woods beyond the Little Camp, it was the life outside that we kept watching. We're on our way toward the life outside.

I'm no longer laughing, I'm singing.

Diego turns around, horrified.

"What do you think you're singing?" he says.

"*La Paloma*, what do you think?"

The hell with him. I think it's perfectly obvious that I'm singing *La Paloma*.

"The hell you say!" and he shrugs his shoulders.

Whenever I sing they tell me to shut up. Even when we sing in unison, I can see the outraged gestures of the others clapping their hands to their ears. So now, when we sing in unison I confine myself to opening my mouth without making a sound. For me it's the only possible solution. But then it's even worse. Even when I'm not singing anything specific, when I'm improvising, they tell me it's off key. I fail to understand how *nothing* can be off key. But apparently, in music, correct pitch and being out of tune are absolute notions. As a result, I can't even sing at the top of my lungs in the shower. Even there they call out to me to shut up.

We walk down the macadam road, saying nothing now. The surrounding countryside is beautiful, but it's empty, it's a lush green landscape in which no one is working, in which not a solitary human figure appears. Perhaps it's not the time for working in the fields, I don't know, I'm from

the city myself. Or maybe that's how it always is, right
after an invasion. Maybe the country is always like that,
empty, warily silent, the day after the invaders have arrived. For us, this is life as it used to be which is beginning
again, life as it used to be before this voyage began. But
for these Thuringian peasants—for, in spite of everything,
there must be some—this is the *after*-life which is beginning
today, the life after the defeat, after the invasion. Perhaps
they're at home, waiting to see what kind of life there will
be after the defeat. I'm curious to know how they'll react to
our arrival in the village.

We reach the first houses at the edge of town. This still
isn't a real street, it's just the extension of the road, with
some houses scattered on either side. These are well-kept
houses, pleasant to behold. From behind a bright white gate
we can hear the barnyard noises. We pass these barnyard
noises without saying a word. And a little farther on is the
village square. It's there all right, we didn't just dream it
up. There's a fountain in the middle, two beeches that provide shade for one corner of the square, with some benches.

The water is flowing into a stone basin polished by the
years, set on a circular terrace with two steps leading up to
it. The water is flowing in an even stream, and occasionally the April wind disperses the stream of water and you
no longer hear the sound of the water falling into the water
below in the basin. We're standing there, watching the
water flow.

Diego goes over to the fountain and takes a long drink.
He stands up, and his face is covered with the glistening
drops.

"It's great," he says.

Then Pierre goes over and drinks.

I look around us at the empty houses fronting on this
square. You would have thought that the village was

empty, but I can feel a human presence behind the closed doors, the closed windows.

Pierre in turn stands up and laughs.

"Jesus, what water!" he says.

At the camp the water was bad, you had to be careful not to drink too much of it. I remember the night we arrived, lots of people became violently ill from having gorged themselves on that tepid, sickening water. The guy from Semur had remained behind in the boxcar. After he had died, I had held him by his arms, I had his corpse against me. But the S.S. opened the sliding doors, their shouts and blows rained down on us, while the police dogs were barking madly. We jumped down onto the platform, barefoot in the winter mud, and I left my pal from Semur behind in the boxcar. I laid his body next to the body of the little old man who had died saying: "What do you know about that!" I was beginning to know something about it, indeed I was.

Haroux also took a drink of that water which was good.

I wonder for how many years that fountain has been spilling its refreshing water. For centuries, probably. Maybe it was the fountain that made this village, this ancient spring which drew the peasants, and the peasant houses, to it. Anyway, I'd be willing to wager that this water was already flowing before the Ettersberg was deforested, when the beeches still covered the slopes where the camp was built. On the esplanade, between the kitchens and the Effektenkammer, the S.S. had saved the beech tree in whose shade, so the story goes, Goethe used to come and sit. I think of Goethe and Eckermann chatting for posterity under this beech tree, between the kitchens and the Effektenkammer. I'm thinking that now they couldn't come there, the tree is all charred and burned inside, now it's nothing but an empty, rotting carcass, an American incendiary bomb liquidated Goethe's beech tree, the day they bombarded the camp kitchens. Haroux is soaking his face in the clear, cool water, and I'm wondering how he would react if I were to tell him that he was drinking Goethe's water, that Goethe surely must have come to this country spring to quench his thirst after having chatted with Eckermann for posterity. I know how he'd react: he'd tell me to fuck off.

Haroux had finished drinking, and it's my turn.

The water is good, no question about it. Not as good as the water of Guadarrama, the water of the springs of the Paular or the Buitrago, but it is good, no question about it. It has a slight metallic aftertaste. At Yerres too, the spring water at the end of the vegetable garden has a slightly ferruginous aftertaste.

We've finished drinking and we're standing there in the middle of the square.

Loitering on the cobblestones of the square, we look around. I wonder if the village is afraid, if the peasants are afraid of us. They've been working in the fields, for years they've seen the buildings of the camp. On Sundays, we used to see them passing by with their wives and children. It was spring, like today, and they were out walking. For us, they were men out walking with their families, after a hard week of work. Their being was immediately accessible, their behavior obvious to us. It was life as it used to be. Our fascinated gaze revealed them in their generic truth. They were peasants, on Sunday, out walking on the road with their families. But how did they perceive us? There must have been some very good reason why we were locked up in a camp, why, winter and summer, they made us work from sunrise, or even before. We were criminals, whose crimes must be particularly heinous. That's how these peasants must have seen us, if indeed they even did see us, if they were really aware of our existence. Actually, they probably never posed the problem of our existence, the problem that our existence posed for them. We no doubt belonged to those events in the world they did not worry about, events they did not have the means to deal with (and besides, they did not care to have the means) as a problem or to think of in terms of problems. War, the criminals on the Ettersberg slope (foreigners to boot, that makes it easier not to worry about it, not to complicate your life), the bombardments, the defeat, and the victories that came before: all these were, literally, events that transcended them. They worked their fields; on Sundays, after having listened to their pastor, they went for a walk, the rest was beyond them. In fact, it's true that the rest was too much for them, since they had decided to let it be too much for them.

"Isn't there anyone in this village?" Pierre says.

"Of course there is, just look around," Haroux replies.

We can, in fact, see that the place is inhabited. The curtains of some of the windows stir. People are peeking out at us. We came here in search of life as it used to be, of life outside. But we've brought with us the threat of everything unknown, of a reality which till yesterday was criminal and punishable. The village feigns emptiness around us.

"All right," Pierre says, "let's get the hell out of here."

He's right, but we remain there loitering on the cobblestones of the square, looking at these houses whose inner life has evaded us. What are we waiting for in this village, actually?

"So?" says Diego. "So it's a German village, there's no use looking so glum about it."

So, we were looking glum. Since Diego says so, we were looking glum. That is, I'm looking glum too, because I can see that the others were looking glum, including Diego.

We laugh, stupidly, and look at each other.

"O.K.," Haroux says, "let's go."

And we leave. The village is expelling us, it's casting out

the sound of our boots, our presence which offends its tranquillity, its ignorant good conscience, it's casting out our striped clothing, our shaved skulls, our Sunday look which used to gaze at the life outside, in this village. And then, in a trice, it wasn't the life outside, it was only another way of being inside, of being inside this same world of systematic oppression, consistent to the very end, of which the camp was the expression. We leave. Still, the water was good, there's no doubt about it. It was cool, it was living water.

"Hey, pal, snap out of it," says the guy from Semur.

Since daybreak, I had sunk into a sort of dull somnolence.

"What?" I ask.

"God! We've been going for hours without stopping, and there you are not seeing a thing. Doesn't the scenery interest you?"

I glance dejectedly out at the scenery. No, for the moment it doesn't interest me. Besides, it's a far cry from yesterday's beauty, from the Moselle valley beneath the snow.

"This scenery isn't beautiful," I say.

The guy from Semur chuckles. That is, I have the feeling he's forcing slightly.

"What would you have preferred?" he says. "An organized tour?"

"I don't prefer anything. It's simply that yesterday it was beautiful, and today the scenery's not beautiful."

Since daybreak, I've been feeling as though my body is about to break into little pieces. I can feel each of these pieces separately, as if my body were no longer whole. The pains in my body scatter to the four corners of the horizon. When I was a child, I remember, in the big barber shop where I used to be taken not far from Bijenkorf, in the Hague, I forced myself to feel the vibrations of the electric clippers in the big mirror opposite me, or the quiver of the razor on my cheeks or the back of my neck. It was a big barber shop for men, with at least ten chairs facing that long mirror which occupied the entire wall. The wires of the electric clippers slid on a sort of triangle at about the height of a man's raised hand. Now that I think of it, it was the same system of clippers sliding on a sort of triangle in the big disinfection room at camp. But here, of course, there weren't any barber's chairs. I used to sit down in the chair in that shop near Bijenkorf and relax. The surrounding warmth, the hum of the clippers, my willful absence from myself, put me into a state of numbness bordering on torpor. Then I shook myself out of it and stared at myself in the long mirror which occupied the entire wall. First I had to concentrate on staring only at my own reflection, isolating it from all the other reflections in the mirror. I had to make sure that the ruddy-faced Dutchman who is having his red beard shaved did not intrude on my efforts. After a moment of almost painful staring, I had the impression that my reflection in the mirror was detaching itself from the polished surface and advancing toward me, or else that it was retreating further, beyond the mirror, but in any event circumscribed by a kind of luminous fringe which isolated me from all the other reflections, which had become hazy, blurred. One final effort, and I no longer felt the vibration of the clippers on my neck, that is, I felt it on my neck, but over there, opposite me, on that neck which must have existed behind the reflection of my head in the mirror. Today, though, I don't have to play, painfully, to banish my bodily feelings; today, all the broken and trampled pieces of my body scatter to the four corners of the tight little horizon of the boxcar. All that remains, all that is really mine, inside myself, is that spongy, burning ball of fire somewhere behind my eyes, in which there seems to reverberate—sometimes slackly, and then suddenly with great intensity—all the aches and pains which reach me from my body, broken into pieces and scattered about me.

"Anyway, we're moving," says the guy from Semur.

Just as he says that, a pale sun is seen reflected on the windows of a signal box, and the train stops beside a station platform.

"Shit," says the guy from Semur.

From all sides, questions stream toward those who are near the opening covered with barbed wire. The guys want to know where we are, what we can see, if it's a station or whether we've stopped again out in the middle of nowhere.

"It's a station," I say for those behind us.

"Does it look like a big city?" someone asks.

"No, it looks more like a small town," the guy from Semur says.

"Are we there?" someone else wants to know.

"How can we tell, pal?" says the guy from Semur.

I look at the station, and out beyond the station, and it does indeed look like a small town. The station platform is empty, and there are guards on the platform and guards barring the doors to the waiting rooms and the entrances onto the platform. We can see people moving behind the windows of the waiting room, behind the turnstiles giving access to the platform.

"Did you see?" I say to the guy from Semur.

He shakes his head. He saw.

"It seems as though we're expected."

The thought that this is perhaps the end of the voyage floats through the fog of my hopeless fatigue. But it doesn't really affect me one way or the other, this thought that perhaps this is the end of the voyage.

"Maybe this is Weimar," says the guy from Semur.

"You're still convinced we're going to Weimar?"

And that we may be at Weimar, that this may be Weimar, doesn't affect me one way or the other. By now I'm nothing but a dull mass, trampled by the gallop of throbbing pain.

"Of course I am, pal," says the guy from Semur, in a conciliatory tone.

And he glances at me. I can see that he thinks it would be best if this were Weimar, that we'd be better off if we actually had arrived. I can see that he thinks I'm at the end of my rope. Nor does the fact that he thinks I can't hold out much longer, that I'm at the end of my rope, affect me in the least.

In Ascona two years later, roughly two years later, I remembered this stop at the provincial station, in the pale light of winter. I had left the train at Solduno, and instead of going straight back up to the house, I remember, I crossed the bridge and walked as far as the Ascona quay. It was winter then too, but the sun was out, I had a coffee on a café terrace in the sun, on the terrace of one of the bistros on the Ascona quay, overlooking the lake which was shimmering in the winter sun. Around me there were women, beautiful women, sports cars, and young men dressed in impeccable flannel. The scenery was lovely, tender, it was the beginning of the postwar period. Around me people were speaking several languages, and the sports cars were honking their horns as they started off with a roar, drowned in laughter, heading for some fleeting pleasure. I was sitting there, I was drinking real coffee, my mind was a blank, that is, the only thought running through it was that soon I would have to leave, that my three months' rest in Italian Switzerland would soon be over. I would have to start organizing my life, that is, I was twenty-two and I had to begin living. During the summer and the autumn of my return I had not yet begun to live. I had simply followed to its conclusion, to its utter limits, every possibility contained in each passing moment. Now I would have to begin to live, to make plans, have a job, obligations, a future. But in Ascona, on the quay in Ascona, beside the lake shimmering in the winter sun, I still didn't have any future. Since my arrival in Solduno, all I had done was soak up sun through every pore in my body and write this book, the only purpose of which, I already knew, was to evolve some semblance of order for myself out of the past. It was then, in Ascona, before my coffee, real coffee, happy in the sunlight, hopelessly happy, an empty, hazy happiness, that I remembered that stop at the little German town during this voyage. As the years went by, I was sometimes assailed by memories, absolutely vivid memories that arose from the willful oblivion of this voyage with the polished perfection of diamonds that nothing can impair. Take tonight, when I was supposed to dine at some friends' house. The table was set in a large, pleasant room, there was a wood fire in the fireplace. We were exchanging small talk, having a pleasant time, and Catherine announced that dinner was ready. She had planned a Russian dinner, and so it was that suddenly I had a piece of black bread in my hand, and mechanically I bit into it, meanwhile continuing the conversation. Then, the slightly acid taste of the black bread, the slow mastication of this gritty black bread, brought back, with shocking suddenness, the marvelous moments when, at camp, we used to eat our ration of bread, when, with Indian-like stealth, we used to stretch it out, so that the tiny squares of wet, sandy bread which we cut out of our daily ration would last as long as possible. I was sitting there motionless, my arm raised, with my slightly acid, buttered slice of good black bread in my hand, and my heart was pounding like a triphammer. Catherine asked me what was the matter. Nothing was the matter, a random thought of no consequence. Obviously I couldn't tell her that I was in the throes of dying, dying of hunger, far far from them, far from the wood fire and the words we were saying, in the snow at Thuringia amid the tall beeches through which the gusts of winter wind were blowing. Or that other time at Limoges, when I was on a trip. We had stopped the car in front of a café called the *Trianon,* across from the Lycée. We were at the bar having a coffee, when someone started up the juke box, that is, I first heard the opening bars of *Tequila* before I realized that someone had started up the juke box. I turned around and saw a group of boys and girls at a table beating time and shaking to the rhythm of *Tequila.* At first I smiled to myself, thinking that you hear *Tequila* played everywhere, actually, and that it was odd to see the well-to-do Limoges youth stomping to the tune of *Tequila.* At first glance, I wouldn't easily have made the connection between Limoges and *Tequila.* I thought of a number of more or less important things regarding the mechanical dissemination of this "canned" music, but I have no intention of trying to reconstruct these more or less important thoughts. The guys were drinking their coffee, maybe they were listening to *Tequila,* they were drinking their coffee, that's all. I turned around again, and this time I noticed the taut, exalted face of that young girl, her eyes closed, an ecstatic mask of *Tequila* transformed into much more than music, into every young girl lost in the limitless world of despair. I took another sip of coffee, the guys weren't saying a word, I wasn't saying anything either, we had driven fourteen hours without stopping, but suddenly I ceased hearing *Tequila* and I could hear very clearly the melody of *Stardust,* the way that Dane who belonged to the jazz combo that Yves had created at camp used to play it on the trumpet. There was no connection, I mean, yes, there was a connection, because it wasn't the same music, but it was the same world of solitude, the same lost, desperate folklore of the Western World. We paid for our coffee, we left, we still had a good stretch of road ahead of us. In Ascona, in the winter sunlight in Ascona, it was that stop in the little German village that came to mind.

The guy from Semur had said: "Hey pal, snap out of it!" just before the train had come to a halt at that little German station, I remember. I lighted a cigarette and tried to figure out why this memory had come to mind. There was no reason for this memory to come to mind, perhaps that's why it came, as a sharp reminder, in the midst of this Ascona sun, this empty fog-shrouded happiness of Ascona, a poignant reminder of this past, of how deep this past was, for perhaps it was the depth of this past which rendered this happiness I experienced in Ascona empty and hazy, as it would with every possible happiness from now on. The fact is that the memory of the little station, the memory of my pal from Semur, came to mind. I was motionless, I was sipping my coffee, again wounded, mortally wounded by the memories of this voyage. The guy from Semur had said: "Hey, pal, snap out of it," and a moment later we had stopped at that German station. Just then a young woman came over to my table. She had pretty painted lips and blue eyes.

"Aren't you a friend of Bob's?" she asked me. I wasn't a friend of Bob's, obviously, how could I be a friend of Bob's? "No," I said, "I'm sorry." "That's too bad," she said, which was a pretty enigmatic remark. "Have you lost Bob?" I asked her. That made her laugh. "Oh, there's no way to lose Bob," she said. Then she sat down on the edge of a chair and took one of my cigarettes, the pack was on the table. She was lovely, rustling, exactly what I needed to forget my pal from Semur. But at that moment I had no desire to forget my pal from Semur. Still, I lighted her cigarette, and I gazed out again over the blue horizon of the lake. The guy from Semur had said: "Anyway, we're moving," or words to that effect, and a moment later the train stopped beside the deserted platform of that German station. "What brings you to these parts?" the young woman asked, "Nothing," I tell her. She gives me an intent look and shakes her head. "In that case, Pat was right," she says. "What does that mean?" I ask her, and yet I haven't the slightest desire to get involved in a conversation with her. "Pat says you're here for no specific reason, for no reason at all, but we think you're hunting for something." I look at her and say nothing. "All right," she says, "I'll leave you to yourself. You live in that circular house up on the Maggia hill, above Solduno." "Is that a question?" I ask her. "Of course not," she says, "I know." "So?" I say. "I'll come by to see you one of these days," she says. "Fine," I tell her, "but make it some evening." She nods her head and gets up. "But don't say anything to Bob," she adds. I shrug my shoulders, I don't know Bob, but she's already gone. I order another coffee and remain in the sun, instead of going back up to the house to work on my book. In any case, I'm going to finish my book because it has to be finished, but I already know it's worthless. Now is not the time for me to tell about this voyage; I have to wait a while, I have to forget this voyage, then later perhaps I'll be able to tell about it.

"Anyway, we're moving," the guy from Semur had said, and a moment later we stopped at that German station, I remembered that in Ascona. Then there was a certain lapse of time, I don't remember now whether it was a matter of minutes or hours, in any case a certain lapse of time, I mean nothing happened for quite a while, we were simply there beside the station platform and the guards were motioning in our direction, no doubt explaining who we were to the crowd that had gathered.

"I wonder what these krauts think of us, how they see us?" says the guy from Semur.

He gazes gravely at that German station and at the German guards and the German curiosity seekers. Actually, it's a fairly intriguing question. Obviously, it's not going to affect us one iota no matter what these Germans massed

behind the waiting-room windows think of us. What we
are, we shall be, no matter how these gaping Germans see
us. But still, we're also what they think they see in us. We
can't completely ignore their stares, which also lay us bare,
which also reveal what we may be. I look at these German
faces, blurred behind the waiting-room windows, and I
remember my arrival at Bayonne seven years before. The
trawler had moored next to the main square, where there
were big beds of flowers and vendors selling vanilla ice
cream. Behind the police barricades, there was a small
crowd of summer vacationers who had come to see us disembark. They saw us as Spanish Reds, and at first this
surprised us, we couldn't understand it, and yet they were
right, we were Spanish Reds, I was already a Spanish Red
without knowing it, and thank God, it's not bad at all,
being a Spanish Red. I'm still a Spanish Red, thank God,
and through the fog of my fatigue I look at that German
station with the eyes of a Spanish Red.

"They see us as gangsters, I suppose, as terrorists," I say
to the guy from Semur.

"In a way," he says, "they're not all that wrong."

"Thank God," I say.

The guy from Semur smiles.

"Thank God," he says. "Can you imagine being in their
shoes?"

I can imagine that we probably wouldn't know we were
in their shoes, I mean we probably would be like them—
brainwashed, convinced that our cause was just.

"You mean to say you prefer being where we are?" I
ask him.

"Well, if you really want to know, I'd prefer being in
Semur. But between them and us, between those krauts
out there looking at us and us, I'd just as soon be here."

The German soldier from Auxerre was another one who,

I felt, would sometimes have preferred to be in my shoes. But I've known others who were quite content to be where they were, they were sure theirs was the best of all possible worlds. Eight days before, coming from Dijon to Compiègne, the two guards assigned to our compartment, for example, hadn't the slightest doubt about the matter. They were two husky fellows in the prime of life who amused themselves by tightening our handcuffs as much as they could and, with their booted feet, giving us a swift kick in the legs. Afterward they would die laughing, they were delighted to be so strong. I was chained to a Pole, a man of about fifty who was convinced we were going to be murdered somewhere along the way. At night, each time the train stopped, he would lean over to me and whisper: "This is it. This time we're all going to get it." At first I had tried to reason with him, but it was useless; he was completely off his rocker. Once, during a prolonged halt, I felt his gasping breath, and he said to me: "You hear that?" I didn't hear a thing, of course, nothing except the breathing of my dozing mates. "What?" I ask him. "The screams," he tells me. No, I didn't hear any screams, there weren't any screams, "What screams?" I ask him. "The screams of the ones being murdered, right there, under the train." I said nothing more, there was no point in saying anything. "You hear that?" he says to me a little while later. I don't react. Then he pulls on the chain that binds us together, wrist to wrist. "The blood," he says, "don't you hear the blood flowing?" His voice was hoarse, a voice no longer human. No, I didn't hear the blood flowing, I heard his crazy voice, I felt my own blood growing cold. "Under the train," he says, "right there under the train, streams of blood, I can hear the blood flowing." His voice grew a trifle louder, and one of the German soldiers growled: "Ruhe, Scheiskerl" and hit him in the chest with the butt of his rifle. The Pole doubled up on the bench; his breathing became a wheeze, but just then the train started off again, and that must have calmed him slightly. I dozed off, and in my half-sleep I kept hearing that no longer human voice speaking of blood, of streams of blood. Today, I sometimes still hear that voice, that echo of ancestral terror, that voice which speaks of the blood of the butchered, that viscous blood itself, which sings dully in the night. Today I sometimes still hear that voice, that distant murmur of the blood in the voice trembling in the wind of madness. Later, at dawn, I was rudely awakened. The Pole was standing up, screaming something I couldn't make out at the German soldiers, his right arm was gesticulating wildly with rage, and the steel of the handcuff was literally sawing my left wrist. Then the Germans began hitting him, till he collapsed into unconsciousness. His face was covered with blood, and his blood had gushed back on me. It was true, now I did hear the blood flowing, long streams of blood flowing onto his clothes, onto the bench, down onto my left hand bound to him by the handcuff. Later they unfastened him, and they dragged him by the feet into the corridor of the car and I strongly suspect he was dead.

I was looking at the German station, where there was still nothing happening, and I was thinking that I'd been traveling now for eight days, including that short stopover at Compiègne. At Auxerre, they got us out of the cells at four in the morning, but we had been forewarned the evening before. Huguette had come by to tell me, she had whispered the news to me through the cell door on her way back to her cell after her stint in the prison kitchens. Huguette had The Mouse wrapped around her little finger, she circulated freely throughout the prison keeping everyone posted. "Tomorrow at dawn there's a departure for Germany, you're in it," she had whispered to me. All right, this is it, we're going to get a look at these notorious camps. The guy from the Othe Forest was dejected. "Dammit," he said, "I would have liked to stay with you, so we could travel together." But he wasn't in this convoy, he was staying behind with Ramaillet. He wasn't exactly overjoyed at the prospect. They took us out of the cells at four A.M.: Raoul, Olivier, three guys from the Hortieux group, and me. It seemed that the whole gallery knew about it, because there was an immediate uproar in the prison, they were calling out to us by our first names and shouting good-bye. They put us on the local train as far as Laroche-Migennes, chained together by twos. At Laroche, we waited on the station platform for the train from Dijon. We were surrounded by six Feldgendarmes, their sub-machine guns at the ready, one for each of us, and there were also two non-coms of the Sicherheitsdienst. We were in a group on the platform, and the passengers passed silently back and forth in front of us. It was cold, my left arm was completely numb, because they had the handcuffs on so tight that there was scarcely any circulation.

"It feels as though we're moving," says the guy from Semur.

He had passed through the Dijon prison a few weeks before me. Dijon is where they assemble the deportees from the whole region before shipping them off to Compiègne.

I look, and we actually do seem to be moving.

"What's that I hear?" someone behind us asks.

The guy from Semur tries to see.

"It sounds as though they're opening the boxcars down the line," he says.

I try to see too.

"Does that mean we're there?" says another voice.

I look and it's true, they're making the guys get down out of the cars at the far end of the platform.

"Can you see?" I ask.

"It looks like the guys are getting right back into the cars," he says.

For several minutes we watch what's happening on the platform.

"Yes, they must be handing out juice, or something like that."

"What do you say, are we there?" they ask behind us.

"It doesn't look like it," says the guy from Semur. "It looks more like they're handing out juice, or something like that."

"Are the guys getting back into the cars?" they ask.

"Yes, they are," I say.

"Jesus, just so long as there's something to drink," someone else says.

They've begun at the back of the train and are moving in our direction.

"We're too far away to see what it is they're handing out," says the guy from Semur.

"Just so it's water," says the same voice as a while back. It must be the guy who's been stuffing himself with sausage throughout the trip, he sounds thirsty as hell.

"We're too far away, we can't see," says the guy from Semur.

Suddenly, there's a noise right next to us, and the German guards take up their station before our car. They must have started the operation at both ends of the convoy. A group of mess cooks move up with big cans and a baggage cart filled with white mess bowls, which look like crockery. We hear the noise of the padlocks and the iron bars, and the boxcar's sliding door opens wide. The guys stop talking; they're waiting. Then there's a stocky S.S. who barks some damn thing and the guys nearest the door begin jumping down onto the station platform.

"That can't be juice they're handing out, not in bowls like that," says the guy from Semur.

We're swept along by the movement toward the door.

"Have to shake a leg," says the guy from Semur, "if we want to keep our places by the window."

We jump down onto the platform and run toward one of the cans in front of which the guys are crowding in great confusion. The S.S. in charge of the operation seem displeased. He must dislike all this commotion and shouting. He must be thinking that, really, these French have no sense of discipline. He screams orders, he pokes his long rubber club more or less at random into the men's backs.

We quickly grab a white bowl—it's crockery all right—and hold it out to the cook. It isn't juice, it's not water, its a sort of brownish broth. The guy from Semur raises the bowl to his mouth.

"The bastards!" he says. "It's as salty as sea water!"

I take a taste, and it's true. It's a thick, salty broth.

"You know what?" says the guy from Semur. "We'd be better off not eating this shit."

I agree, and we're about to set down our full bowls. There's a wide-eyed German soldier watching us do it.

"Was ist denn los?" he says. He wants to know what's going on.

I show him the bowls and tell him:

"Viel zu viel Salz." There's much too much salt.

He stands there gaping and shaking his head as he watches us leave. He must think we're pretty damn difficult.

As we're about to climb back into our boxcar, we hear a terrible din: whistles blowing, shrill laughter and exclamations. I turn around, so does the guy from Semur. A group of German civilians has made its way onto the platform. Men and women both. They must be the local V.I.P.'s, whom they're allowing to witness the spectacle at close quarters. They were laughing so hard they were crying; they were gesturing broadly, and the women were clucking hysterically. We try to see what has them all worked up.

"Oh, Christ!" says the guy from Semur.

The men two cars down from us are stark naked. They are hopping up onto the platform, trying to cover themselves with their hands, all of them without a stitch of clothing on.

"What kind of a circus is this?" I ask.

The Germans are enjoying themselves royally. Especially the civilians. The women inch over closer to the spectacle of all these naked men running grotesquely along the station platform, and now they're chortling louder than ever.

"That must be the car that some people escaped from," says the guy from Semur. "Instead of simply taking off their shoes, they stripped them naked."

Yes, that must be it, of course.

"Those bitches are really having a ball," says the guy from Semur disgustedly.

Then we climb back into the car. But there are a fair number of other guys who must have done what we did, who hurried back, and the places near the window are already taken. Still, we push our way over as close as possible.

"It's damn pathetic," he says, "making a spectacle of yourself like that."

If I understand correctly, he's put out by the guys who jumped down onto the platform naked. And, actually, he's right.

"I mean for Christ's sake," he says, "knowing that these bitches were going to get a charge out of it, they could have stayed in their car."

He shakes his head, highly displeased.

"Some people just don't know how to behave," he concludes.

Once again he's right. When you start off on a journey like this you have to know how to behave and know what the score is. And it's not only a question of dignity, it's also a practical matter. When you know how to act and what the score is, you have a better chance of holding out. There's no question about it, you hold out better. Later, I had a chance to verify how right my pal from Semur was. When he said that in that German train station, I thought that, in general, he was right, I thought that, yes, one has to know how to act in a journey such as this. But it was only later that I realized the full practical importance of the matter. Later, in the Little Camp—the quarantine section—I often thought of the guy from Semur as I watched the way the Colonel was acting. The Colonel was some important personage in De Gaulle's Resistance Movement, or so the story went, and it must have been true, because subsequently he made a name for himself, he became a General, I've often seen his name in the papers, and each time I smiled to myself. In the quarantine camp, the Colonel had become a bum. He really didn't know how to behave, he had stopped washing, he would stoop to anything for a second helping of stinking soup. Later, when I saw the picture of the Colonel—then a General—published on the occasion of some official ceremony, I couldn't help thinking of the guy from Semur, of the truth of his starkly simple words. How true it is that some people don't know how to behave.

The guys are climbing back into the boxcar now; whistles are blown down on the station platform, voices are shouting orders, a great din. It seems that the fact of having been able to stretch their arms and legs, if only for a few minutes, has made the men lose their already acquired habit of being stacked in against one another. They're protesting, shouting: "For Christ's sake, stop shoving!" to the latecomers trying to force their way into the doughlike mass of bodies. But the latecomers are being shoved into the car beneath a hail of kicks and blows, they have to shoulder their way in. "We're not going to stay on the platform, dammit," they shout back. The sliding door slams shut and the viscous welter of bodies continues to stir for several minutes, with grunts and sudden outbursts of blind fury. Then, progressively, calm is restored, the bodies settle back into their overlapping pattern, the mass of bodies crammed together in the shadow resumes its gasping, whispering life, oscillating to the jolts of the voyage.

The guy from Semur is still in a foul mood because of these characters two cars down from us who made a spectacle of themselves. And I understand his point of view. As long as the Germans, on the station platform and behind the waiting-room windows, pictured us as gangsters, as terrorists, there was no problem. For they were thus seeing what was essential or vital in us, the essence of our truth, that is, that we were the implacable enemies of their world, their society. The fact that they took us for criminals was secondary. Their good, brainwashed conscience was secondary. The main point was indeed the implacable nature of our relationship, the fact that we and they were the opposing terms of an insoluble relationship, that we were the mutual negation of each other. It was normal, and even desirable, for them to hate us, for their hate endowed what we had done, the essence of the acts which had brought us to this train, with a clear meaning. But that they were able to witness the grotesque spectacle of those naked men cavorting like monkeys in pursuit of a bowl of disgusting broth was a serious matter. It falsified the fair relationship of hate and absolute opposition between them and us. That hysterical laughter of the women in the presence of those naked men leaping about on the station platform was like an acid eating at the very essence of our truth. So there was good reason for the guy from Semur to be in a foul mood.

"Well, the voyage goes on," I say.

The guy from Semur looks at me and shakes his head.

"We'll hold out till it's over, pal," he says.

"Sure we will," I reply.

"Till it's over, and then some," he says.

"Sure we will."

I look at him, and I'm convinced that he will indeed hold out. The guy from Semur is solid, on important matters he thinks straight, he'll hold out. Sometimes his ideas are a trifle over-simplified, but actually one can't blame him for that. I look at him, and I'm convinced he'll hold out. And yet he's going to die. At dawn after this next night, he's going to die. He's going to say: "Don't leave me, pal," and he's going to die.

Two years later, roughly two years later, in Ascona, I'm finishing my second cup of coffee and thinking how lousy it is that the guy from Semur is dead. There's no one left to whom I can talk about this voyage. It's as though I'd made this voyage all alone. Henceforth, I'm all alone, when I remember this voyage. The solitude of this voyage is probably going to prey on me for the rest of my life. I pay and start slowly away, here on the quay in Ascona, in the winter sunlight in Ascona. I cross the bridge and walk toward Solduno. I'll have to cope with it myself, the guy from Semur is dead.

I was also struck like a slap in the face by my solitude as I left that German house, after we had drunk some water from the fountain on the square of that German village. Haroux, Pierre, Diego and I were walking back toward the camp, we were walking in silence, and we still hadn't seen a living soul. We saw the contour of the camp before us now, we were seeing the camp as the peasants must have seen it for years. Because they did see the camp, for Christ's sake, they actually did see it, they had to see what was going on, even if they didn't want to know. In three or four days the Americans are going to take several contingents of Weimar residents to the camp. They are going to show them the quarantine camp, filled with the stench of the ill and infirm, who are still dying. They're going to show them the crematorium, the section where the German S.S. doctors carried out their experiments on the prisoners, they're going to show them Ilse Koch's lampshades made out of human skin, the ravishing parchment lampshades on which can be seen the blue lines of the tattoos etched on human skin. Then the women from Weimar, in their new spring finery, and the men from Weimar, with their professor- and grocer-like glasses, will start to cry, start to scream that they didn't know, that they aren't responsible. I must say, the spectacle turned my stomach, I retreated into a corner by myself, I fled and buried my face in the spring grass, amid the murmur of spring in the trees.

Sigrid didn't know either, or maybe she didn't want to know, rather. I used to see her in the neighborhood bistros, we used to exchange an occasional word. I believe she was a model for some women's magazines. And I had forgotten the Weimar women, in their spring dresses, gathered in front of Block 50, listening to the American officer explaining to them Ilse Koch's pleasures before taking them in to see the dainty tattoos on the parchment-like human skin, the lampshades that Ilse Koch used to collect. I believe I had forgotten everything, and when I saw Sigrid in the neighborhood bistros I used to look at her and find her beautiful. One evening, though, we chanced to be at the same table, and it just so happened, on that particular evening, that I felt as though I were awaking from a dream, as though life, since my return from this voyage ten years before, had been nothing but a dream. Maybe I hadn't yet had too much to drink when I noticed Sigrid at the same table, but the signs were out that I was going to drink too much. Or maybe, quite simply, drink had nothing whatever to do with it, maybe there was no point in looking for some external, accidental reason for that anxiety which welled up once again. Anyway, I was having a drink, I heard the hubbub of conversation, and I saw Sigrid.

"Guten Abend, Sigrid, wie geht's Dir?" I said to her.

She has short hair and green eyes. She looks at me with surprise.

"Du sprichst Deutsch?" she says.

I smile; of course I know German.

"Selbstverständlich," I tell her.

It doesn't go without saying that I know German, but anyway, I tell her it goes without saying.

"Wo hast Du's gelernt?" the girl asks.

"Im Kazett."

It's not true that I learned German in the camp, I already knew it before, but anyway I feel like giving the girl a hard time.

"Wo denn?" she says with surprise. She obviously didn't understand.

Obviously, she doesn't know that these two initials, KZ, stand for her country's concentration camps, that this is how her own countrymen, who had spent ten or twelve years in the camps, had designated them. Maybe she never heard a word about the whole thing.

"Im Konzentrationslager. Schon davon gehört?" I ask her.

I ask her point-blank whether she's ever heard of the concentration camps, and she looks at me closely. She takes a cigarette and lights it.

"What's the matter with you?" she says, in French.

"Nothing."

"Why are you asking these questions?"

"In order to find out," I tell her.

"Find out what?"

"Everything. It's too easy not to know," I tell her.

She smokes and says nothing.

"Or to forget. It's too easy to forget."

She smokes.

"For example, you might just be Dr. Haas' daughter," I tell her.

She shakes her head.

"I'm not Dr. Haas' daughter," she says.

"But you might be his daughter."

"Who's Dr. Haas?" she wants to know.

"I hope it's 'was.' "

"Then who was Dr. Haas?"

"A character from the Gestapo," I tell her.

She snuffs out her half-smoked cigarette and looks at me.

"Why are you treating me like this?" she says.

"I'm not treating you, I'm asking you."

"Do you think you can treat me like this?" she says.

"I don't think anything. I'm asking you."

She takes another cigarette and lights it.

"Go on," she says. And she looks me straight in the eye.

"Your father's not Dr. Haas?"

"No," she answers.

"He wasn't in the Gestapo?"

"No," she says.

She doesn't avert her gaze.

"Maybe in the Waffen-S.S.," I tell her.

"Not that either."

"And he was never a Nazi, of course," I say.

At that point I burst out laughing, I can't help laughing.

"I don't know."

Suddenly I've had enough.

"That's true," I say, "you don't know anything. Nobody knows anything any more. There never was any Gestapo, never any Waffen-S.S., never any Totenkopf. I must have been dreaming."

This evening I no longer know whether I dreamed all that, or whether I've been dreaming since the whole thing has ceased to exist.

"Tonight, wake not those who are sleeping," I say.

"What's that?" Sigrid wants to know.

"It's a poem."

"A very short poem, no?" she says.

And then I smile at her.

"Die deutsche Gründlichkeit, die deutsche Tatsächlichkeit. And the hell with German qualities."

She blushes slightly.

"You've been drinking," she says.

"I'm just beginning to."

"Why me?" she asks.

"You?"

"Why pick on me?"

I take a drink from the new glass they've just set in front of me.

"Because you are oblivion, because your father was never a Nazi, because there were never any Nazis. Because they didn't kill Hans. Because we shouldn't have awakened the sleepers tonight."

She shakes her head.

"You're going to drink too much," she says.

"I never drink enough."

I finish my glass and order another.

People are coming in and leaving, girls are laughing too loudly, there's music, the sound of glasses, a real mob, this dream you find yourself in when you awake. Have to do something.

"Why are you sad?" Sigrid asks.

I shrug my shoulders.

"I'm not sad," I say. "What does it mean, to be sad?"

"Well, unhappy."

"What does it mean to be happy?"

"Unhappy, I didn't say happy, I said unhappy," she says.

"It's the same thing, isn't it?"

"Of course not."

"In reverse, the same thing in reverse, I mean."

"Absolutely not," Sigrid says.

"You surprise me, Sigrid. You're not Dr. Haas' daughter, and you know all sorts of things."

But she doesn't let me change the subject.

"They aren't two different sides of the same coin," she says. "Happiness and unhappiness are quite different, made up of many different things."

"What is happiness, Sigrid?" and as I ask the question I wonder if I would really be able to define the term.

She takes a puff on her cigarette and pauses to think.

"It's when you realize that you really exist," she says.

I take a drink of liquor and look at her.

"It's when the certainty of living becomes so acute that you feel like shouting," she says.

"Maybe out of pain," I say.

Her green-eyed gaze, directed squarely at me, is filled with amazement. As if it were impossible for her to conceive that the certainty of living, in all its fullness, could have the slightest connection with the pain of living.

"On Sundays, for example," I tell her.

She waits for the rest, which doesn't come.

"Warum am Sonntag?" she pursues.

Perhaps it's true that she knows nothing, perhaps it's true that she doesn't even suspect the reality of Sundays, at the edge of the little wood, beside the electrified barbed wire, the village beneath its quiet smoke, the winding road and the green, fertile Thuringian plain.

"Come on and dance, I'll explain the meaning of happiness to you later."

She gets up and smiles, shaking her head.

"You can't know anything about that," she says.

"About what?"

"Happiness," she says, "what happiness means."

"Why not?"

"You just can't know, that's all."

"Sure I do. It's the Moselle valley."

"You see," Sigrid says, "you spend all your time remembering."

"Not all my time. I spend all my time trying to forget."

"It doesn't matter," she says. "Remembering, forgetting, it's the past that matters."

"So what?"

We're walking over toward the part of the room where you can dance.

"I've already told you, happiness is always a question of the present, of now."

She's in my arms and we're dancing and I feel like laughing.

"You're just what the doctor ordered."

She's in my arms and it's the present and I'm thinking that she must have left her country, her family, no doubt because of the burden of this past of which she wants no part, not the slightest part, neither for good nor evil, for revenge or for the example, this past that she is merely trying to erase, through an infinite succession of meaningless gestures, of days without roots in any soil nourished by ancient acts, nothing but days and nights, days succeeding nights, and here of course, in these bars, among the futilely uprooted people, no one calls her to account, no one cares about the truth of her past or her family's past, or her country's, she could, in all innocence, be Dr. Haas' daughter, who models for women's magazines, who goes out dancing in the evening, who is happy and lives in the acute certainty of being alive.

"Ever been to Arosa?"

She shakes her head, no.

"It's in Switzerland, in the mountains," I tell her.

"Everything in Switzerland is in the mountains," she says with a knowing pout.

I have to admit she's right.

"So?" she says.

"At Arosa, there's a chalet in the mountains with a beautiful inscription in Gothic letters engraved on the façade."

But Sigrid doesn't seem to be especially interested in the multi-colored inscription in Gothic letters shining in the mountain sunlight at Arosa.

"Glück und Unglück, beides trag in Ruh'—alles geht vorüber und auch Du. Take happiness and unhappiness in your stride—for everything passes away, even you."

"Is that your inscription?" she asks.

"Yes."

"I don't like it."

The music has stopped, and we're waiting for them to put on another record.

"Maybe you should take happiness in your stride," says Sigrid, "and even that's assuming a good deal. You shouldn't take it in your stride anyway, you ought to grab it. But what about unhappiness? How can anyone take that in stride?"

"I don't know," I say, "but that's what the inscription says."

"It's stupid. And don't you find that to say that everything passes away is a lot of empty nonsense?"

"I can see you don't appreciate that noble thought."

"No, your thing's phony," she says.

"It's not mine; it's a beautiful Gothic inscription at Arosa, in the mountain sunlight."

We start to dance again.

"Actually, the contrary is true."

"We can try," I say.

"Try what?"

"Try to reverse that noble thought and see what comes out."

We're dancing slowly, and she smiles.

"All right," she says.

"Glück und Unglück, beides trag in Unruh'—alles bleibt in Ewigkeit, nicht Du. Worry about happiness and unhappiness—for everything is eternal, except you. That's what we'd get."

She reflects and frowns.

"I don't like that either," she says.

"So?"

"So nothing. The opposite of something stupid is never anything except something stupid."

We both laugh.

When this evening is over, and when I recall this evening during which, suddenly, the acute memory of this forgotten past, this past so perfectly buried in my memory, waked me from the dream which was my life, when later I shall try to relate this chaotic evening, into which events intruded which were perhaps futile but which to me seemed charged with meaning, I'll realize that Sigrid, the green-eyed German girl, assumes a special significance in the story, I'll realize that, imperceptibly, Sigrid becomes the focal point of that evening, and, later, of that night. Perhaps it's quite natural for Sigrid to assume a special significance in my story, because she is, or is trying with all her might to be, the oblivion of this past which cannot be forgotten, the will to forget this past which nothing can ever erase but which Sigrid rejects, from herself, her life, from all the lives around her, with her happiness of every passing moment, her acute certainty of being alive, as opposed to the acute certainty of death which oozes out of this past like some bitter, bracing resin. Perhaps this importance, this etching needle emphasizing the character of Sigrid in the story which, if I have to, I may tell of this evening, Sigrid's suddenly obsessive importance derives merely from the extreme, the burning tension which she personifies, between the weight of this past and the refusal to remember this past, as if her smooth face, washed by centuries of slow, Nordic rains which, having polished and softly molded her eternally fresh, pure face, her body perfectly suited to the appetite for juvenile perfection which vibrates within each of us and which must have aroused in every man who had eyes to see, that is, eyes that were really open, really disposed to let themselves be touched by the reality of existing things, must have aroused in all of them a desperate desire for possession, as if this face and body, reproduced tens, perhaps thousands of times in the women's magazines, were there only in order to make us forget the body and face of Ilse Koch, that straight, stocky body planted solidly on her straight, sturdy legs, that harsh, sharp, incontestably German face, those fair eyes, like Sigrid's eyes (but neither the photographs nor the newsreels taken at the time, and since used and re-used in certain films, enabled anyone to ascertain whether Ilse Koch's fair eyes were green like Sigrid's, or blue or light blue or iron gray—more likely iron gray), Ilse Koch's eyes fixed on the naked torso, on the bare arms of the deportee she had chosen as her lover a few hours before, her gaze already cutting out that white, sickly skin along the dotted lines of the tattoo which had caught her attention, her gaze already picturing the handsome effect of those bluish lines, those flowers or sailing ships, those snakes, that seaweed, that long female hair,

those pinks of the wind, those sea waves and those sailing
vessels, again those sailing vessels deployed like screaming
gulls, their handsome effect on the parchment-like skin—
having, by some chemical process, acquired an ivory tint—of
the lampshades covering every lamp in her living room
where, at dusk, she had smiled at the deportee brought in
first as the chosen instrument of pleasure, a twofold pleasure, first in the act of pleasure itself and then for the much
more durable pleasure of his parchment-like skin, properly
treated, the color of ivory, crisscrossed by the bluish lines
of the tattoo which gave the lampshade its inimitable
stamp, there, reclining on a couch, she assembled the officers of the Waffen-S.S. about her husband, the Commandant
of the camp, to listen to one of them play some romantic
melody on the piano, or something serious from the piano
repertory, a Beethoven concerto perhaps; as if the laughter
of this girl, Sigrid, whom I was holding in my arms, this
laughter which was so young and full of promise, existed
only to efface, to relegate to total oblivion, the other
laughter of Ilse Koch reflecting her pleasure, the double
pleasure of the moment itself and of the lampshade which
would remain as evidence, like shells gathered at the sea-
shore on a week-end, or dried flowers, in memory of the
pleasure of the moment itself.

But at the start of this evening, before we meet François
and the others, before we've joined forces with them to go
on together to another nightclub, I still don't know that
Sigrid will assume such significance in the story I shall tell
of that evening. In fact, I'm still trying to decide to whom
I could tell the story of that evening. I have Sigrid in my
arms and I'm thinking about happiness. I'm thinking that
till now I have never done anything, I have never decided
anything, in terms of the happiness or unhappiness I might
derive from it. If anyone were to ask me whether I had
thought of the happiness that such and such an act which

I had decided upon might procure me, I'd find the notion laughable, as if there were a reserve of happines somewhere, a kind of storehouse from which one could draw, perhaps, as if happiness were not something that comes, even in the depths of the most profound distress, the most dreadful destitution, after one has done exactly what one has had to do.

And perhaps happiness is nothing more than this feeling I experienced after I had fled from the spectacle of the tearful Weimar women gathered in front of Block 50, when I buried my face in the spring grass, on the other side of the Ettersberg slope, with the spring trees all around. There was the silence and the trees, without end. The faint murmurs of silence and of the wind in the trees, a flood of silence and faint sounds. And then, in my anguish, mingled with my anguish, I had a distinct feeling, like the song of a bird mingled with the silence, that I had spent my twenty years the way they had to be spent, and that perhaps I still had another twenty, or twice twenty, to keep on doing what had to be done.

I also lay down on the grass and gazed for a long time at the Ettersberg landscape after leaving that German house.

That house stood slightly apart, on the edge of the village.

I noticed that house when Haroux, Diego, Pierre and I were on our way back to camp. It was a fairly well-to-do house. But what struck me, what froze me to the spot, was the realization that it was so placed that its windows offered a perfect view of the entire camp. I looked at the windows, looked at the camp, and I said to myself that I had to go into that house, I had to meet the people who had lived there all these years.

"Hey," I had shouted to the others, "I'm staying here."

"What do you mean, you're staying here?" Pierre asked, turning around.

The other two also turned around and looked at me.

"What's the matter with you now?" Haroux asks.

"Nothing's the matter," I say.

"You see a girl in the window?" Pierre asks mockingly.

I shrug my shoulders.

"Then for Christ's sake," Haroux says, "if you don't want to rape a girl what the hell do you want in that house?"

I light a cigarette and look at the house, I look at the camp. Diego follows my gaze and smiles wryly, as he always does.

"Bueno, Manuel, y que?" O.K., Manuel. So what about it?

"Has visto?"

"He visto, y qué le vas a hacer?"

He's seen what I've seen, but he wants to know what I can do about it.

"Come on, you two," Haroux shouts, "can't you talk like everyone else, so we can follow the conversation."

"Don't be so so chauvinistic," Diego says, "not everybody speaks French, you know."

"But we happen to be here," Haroux says, "and we'd like to know what's going on."

"Listen," Diego says, "you have any idea how many million people speak Spanish?"

"Come on, that's enough," Haroux says, "no sermons, please."

Diego laughs.

"Fair enough," he says, "I just wanted to make a point. Not everyone in the world speaks French."

"So why does Gérard want to go into that house?" Pierre wants to know.

Diego shrugs his shoulders.

"Ask him," he says.

So Pierre asks me:

"Why in the hell do you want to visit that house anyway?"

"You see where it is?" I tell them.

They look at the house, then turn around and look at the camp.

"Jesus Christ!" Haroux exclaims, "how right you are, they had first-row seats."

Pierre shakes his head and says nothing. He looks at me.

"So where does that get you?" Haroux asks.

I don't know. Frankly, I haven't the slightest idea where that gets me.

"I just want to look around," I say.

"If it's for kicks," Haroux says, shrugging his shoulders.

"No," I say, "it's not for kicks."

Diego looks at me and smiles again.

"Bueno," he says, "luego nos vemos, Manuel. Come on, boys, he'll tell us all about it."

They wave a vague good-bye and leave.

Then I go over to the house. I push open the gate of the fence surrounding the little garden in front of the house and go in. At the end of the path I go up three steps and knock on the front door.

At first no one comes. Then I start banging on the door with my fist and kicking the lower part violently with my boot. A moment later, I hear a woman's voice behind the door.

"Aufmachen," I shout, "los aufmachen!"

I realize I'm screaming like an S.S. "Los" was the key word in the S.S. vocabulary. I feel like dropping the whole thing and taking off to catch up with my mates. But it's too late, the door is already ajar. There's an elderly woman with graying hair standing in the opening, looking at me with a worried air. She doesn't look as though she's afraid, merely worried, wondering what I want.

"Ich bin allein," she says. I'm all alone.

"Ich auch." Me too.

She glances at what I'm wearing and asks what I want.

"Ich möchte das haus besuchen." I tell her I want to look

around her house, that she has nothing to fear from me. I simply want to visit her house.

She doesn't seem afraid, she is simply wondering why I want to look around her house, but finally she opens the door and lets me in.

I walk slowly through the downstairs rooms, with the woman at my heels. She doesn't say a word, nor do I. I look at these ordinary rooms in this ordinary country house. It isn't exactly a country house, it's a house which belongs to people who live in the country. I wonder what the people in this house do for a living.

Actually, I'm not interested in the downstairs rooms. Because the good view of the camp must be from the upstairs rooms. An unobstructed view. I walk quickly from room to room, with the gray-haired woman at my heels. I'm looking for the stairway leading to the second story. I find that stairway and go up to the second story. The woman paused for a second at the foot of the stairs and watched me go up. She must be wondering what I want, yes, that's surely what she's wondering. Besides, she wouldn't understand if I explained to her that all I want is a look. I'm not hunting for anything except to look. To look, from outside, at that enclosure in which we've been caged for years. Nothing else. If I were to tell her that that was what I want, merely that, she wouldn't understand. How could she? To understand this physical need to look at it from the outside, you have to have been inside. She can't understand, no one on the outside can understand. Going up the stairs to the second story of the house, I vaguely wonder whether this need to look, from outside, at the inside in which we were caged doesn't mean I'm slightly deranged. Maybe I've gone slightly off my rocker, as the saying goes. A possibility not to be dismissed. Maybe that's why Diego had that wry smile. Let him satisfy his little whims: maybe that's what he meant by his wry smile. For the moment that doesn't worry me. I feel like looking from the outside, it's not all that serious. It can't do anyone any harm. That is, it can't harm anyone but me.

I reach the top of the stairway and pause before the three doors that open onto the landing. But the gray-haired woman has overtaken me and takes the lead. She pushes one of the doors.

"Das ist die Wohnstube," she says.

I told her I wanted to visit her house, so she's showing it to me. She opens a door and tells me that this is the living room. The gray-haired woman is most obliging.

I go into the living room and yes, it's just what I expected. No, if I'm honest I have to say that although this is what I expected, I was hoping it would be different. It was a ridiculous hope, of course, for unless the camp were eliminated, expunged from the landscape, it couldn't be different. I go over to the living room windows and see the camp. Framed in one of the windows I see the square chimney of the crematorium. So I look. I wanted to see, and I'm seeing. I'd like to be dead, but I'm seeing, I'm alive and I'm seeing.

Behind me, the gray-haired woman is saying:

"Eine gemütliche Stube, nicht wahr?"

I turn back toward her, but I can't see her, I can't manage to fix her image or the image of that room. How does one translate "gemütlich"? I try to grapple with this minor, concrete little problem, but I can't, I slide over this concrete little problem, I slide into the pressing, woolly problem framed by one of the windows: the looming crematorium chimney. If Hans were here in my place, what would he do? Surely he woudn't let himself founder in this nightmare.

"Did you used to spend your evenings in this room?" I ask.

She looks at me.

"Yes," she says, "we spend our evenings in this room."

"Have you lived here for a long time?"

"Oh yes!" she says, "a very long time."

"In the evening," I ask her, but in fact it's not a question, since there can't be the slightest doubt about it, "in the evening, when the flames shot up beyond the crematorium chimney, could you see the crematorium flames?"

She gives a sudden start and clutches at her neck with one hand. She takes a step backward, and now she's afraid. Till now she hasn't been afraid, but now she is.

"Both my sons," she says, "both my sons were killed in the war."

She throws the bodies of her two sons at me for fodder, she takes refuge behind the lifeless bodies of her two sons killed in the war. She's trying to make me believe that all suffering is the same, that all the dead weigh the same. As a counter-balance for all my dead friends, for the weight of their ashes, she's offering the weight of her own suffering. But all the dead don't weigh the same, of course. No corpse of the German army will ever weigh as much as the smoke of one of my dead companions.

"I hope so, I really hope they're dead."

She retreats another step, until her back is smack against the wall.

I'm going to leave. I'm going to leave this room—how does one translate "gemütlich"?—I'm going back out into the spring sunshine, back to my friends, back to my prison, I'm going to try and talk with Walter tonight, he's been imprisoned for twelve years, for twelve years he's been softly chewing the black bread of the camps with his jaw that the Gestapo fractured, for twelve years he's been sharing the black bread of the camps with his pals, for twelve years he's been smiling his invincible smile. I remember that Walter was crying with happiness, because this defeat of his country could mean the victory of his country. He was crying with joy, because he knew that now he could die. I mean, now he not only had reasons for living, but also reasons for having lived. In '39, in '40, in '41, the S.S. used to assemble them on the main square, at attention, so they could listen to the victory communiqués of the German General Command. In those days, Walter told me, he gritted his teeth and swore he would hold out till the end, no matter what. And he had held out. Most of them were dead, and even the survivors were mortally wounded, they'll never be alive like the others, but they had held out. Walter was crying with happiness, he had held out, he had been worthy of himself, of that concept of life he had chosen so long ago in a Wuppertal factory. I had to find Walter, I had to talk to him that evening.

The gray-haired woman is hugging the wall and looking at me.

I haven't the strength to tell her that I understand her sorrow, that I respect her sorrow. I understand that for her the death of both her sons is the most atrocious, the most unjust thing in the world. I haven't the strength to tell her that I understand her sorrow, but that I'm happy both her sons are dead, I mean I'm happy the German Army is wiped out. I haven't the strength to tell her all that.

I walk past her and run down the stairs, run through the garden and on up the road toward the camp, toward my friends.

"No, no," says the guy from Semur, "you never told me that story."

And yet I was sure I had talked to him about it. Since the train had left that German station, we had been moving along at a good clip. The guy from Semur and I had in fact reached the point of exchanging stories about our life in the maquis.

"I never told you the story of the motorcycle?" I ask him.

"No, man, you never did."

So I tell him, and, in fact, he clearly remembers that motorcycle which had remained in the sawmill the night the Germans took them by surprise.

"You were out of your minds," he says, when I explain to him how Julien and I went back for the motorcycle.

"Maybe we were, but it really made Julien sick to think that that motorcycle was lost."

"Completely out of your minds," he says. "Who's this Julien anyway?"

"I already told you about him."

"The guy from Laignes?" he asks.

"That's right: Julien. He really wanted that motorcycle."

"Damn stupid, if you ask me," says the guy from Semur.

"You said it," I agree.

"They must have had a gay old time taking pot shots at you," he says.

"They did indeed. But Julien wanted that motorcycle."

"Crazy idea," he says. "It's not as though there weren't any other motorcycles."

"But he wanted that particular one," I insist.

"It's stupidities like that that get you killed," says the guy from Semur.

How well I know.

"What did you do with it?" he asks.

I tell him how we drove it to the Taboo underground in the hills between Laignes and Chatillon. The autumn trees along the road were yellow and gold. There was a car belonging to the Feld parked at an intersection just beyond Montbard, and the four German gendarmes were pissing in the ditch.

The guy from Semur bursts out laughing.

"What did they do?"

When they heard the noise of the motorcycle, they turned

around, all four of them at the same time, like mechanical dolls. Julien jammed on the brakes, and they saw we were armed.

"You should have seen them taking off into the ditch, without even pausing to button their flies."

The guy from Semur laughs again.

"Did you fire at them?" he asks.

"Hell no, we didn't want to stir up the whole region. We took off."

"But in the end they got you anyway," says the guy from Semur.

"Not Julien."

"But they got you anyway," he persists.

"Later," I say, "much later. Pure chance, there was nothing I could do about it."

"Pure chance" isn't quite exact. It was one of the predictable, rational, compelling consequences of what we were doing. What I meant was that the way it happened, the circumstances of the arrest itself, were due in part to chance. It might have happened quite differently, it might never even have happened at all, at least when it did: that's what I meant. It was by chance that I was arrested at Joigny that particular day. I was on my way back from Laroche-Migennes, where I had again tried to make contact with the group that had blown up the munitions train at Pontigny. Actually, I should have gone straight back to Paris to rejoin Michel. But it so happened that I was sleepy, I was several nights behind in my sleep. So I stopped off in Joigny at Irène's house, just to catch a few hours sleep. Just in time to be caught by the Gestapo. The next day, at Auxerre, there were roses in Dr. Haas' garden. They took me out into the garden, and I saw the roses. Dr. Haas didn't come with us, he remained behind in his office. There was only the tall one with the blond hair, who looked as though he used make-up, and the fat one who was stationed in

Joigny with Haas, the one who was always short of breath.
They made me walk in the garden that belonged to the
house, and I saw the roses. They were beautiful. I had
time enough to think how strange it was that I should
notice the roses and find them beautiful, knowing what they
were going to do to me. From the start, I had carefully concealed the fact that I understood German. They talked
openly in front of me, which gave me a few seconds—however long it took them to translate—to prepare myself for
what was coming next. They took me to a tree in the
garden, beside the bed of roses, and I already knew that
they were going to suspend me from a branch by slipping
a rope between the handcuffs, and then loose the dog on
me. The dog, held in tow by the tall blond who looked as
though he used make-up, was growling and straining at his
leash. Later, a lot later, I looked at the roses through the
fog in front of my eyes. I tried to forget my body and the
pain that racked my body, I tried to make an abstraction
of my body and all the feelings convulsing my body, by
looking at the roses, by filling my eyes with roses. Just as
I succeeded, I passed out.

"They all say that," says the guy from Semur.

"They all say what?" I ask him.

"That it was a question of chance, that there was nothing
they could do about it," says the guy from Semur.

"Sometimes it's true."

"Perhaps," he says, "but they always end by getting
caught."

"The ones who are caught always find that people always
end by getting caught."

The guy from Semur reflects for a moment on that truism.

"There you're right," he says, "for once you're right. Have
to check the opinion of the ones who haven't been caught."

"That's the way to reason."

He shrugs his shoulders.

"It's easy enough to reason," he says, "but meanwhile here we are like rats in a trap."

"This camp we're going to," I ask him, "since you seem to know all about it, what do people do there?"

"Work," he says, quite sure of himself.

"Doing what?" I want to know.

"You're asking too much," he says, "all I know is they work."

I try to picture what kind of work they can do in a camp. But I can't imagine the reality, as I was later to know it. Actually, it's not because of any lack of imagination, it's simply that, from the facts available to me, I was unable to draw complete conclusions. The basic point is that we are the labor force. Insofar as we have not been shot immediately after our arrest, and also insofar as we do not fall into the category of those blindly, ineluctably slated for extermination, as the Jews are, we've become the labor force. A special kind of manpower, to be sure, since we are not free to sell our talents, we are not obliged to sell our labor power on the open market. The S.S. don't buy our ability, they simply extort it from us, through a wholly unjustifiable coercion, through pure violence. For the basic point is that we are the labor force. The only thing is, since our labor power has not been bought, there is no economic necessity to insure its reproduction. As soon as our labor power is exhausted, the S.S. will go out and look for some more.

Today, seventeen years after this voyage, if I recall that day seventeen years ago when, in the course of the voyage, I tried to picture what kind of life might exist in a camp, I see various images superimposed, several successive layers of images. Thus when a plane is descending to land, it sometimes happens that it passes through several layers of cloud formations—some of which are thick and heavy, others fleecy, laterally lighted by the slanting rays of an invisible sun—it sometimes happens that between two layers of clouds, the plane finds a free fringe of blue sky above the woolly formations that we will later pass through on our way down to solid ground. Today, when I think back on all that, several layers of images, stemming from various places and times in my life, are superimposed. There are, first of all, the images which were etched in my memory during the two weeks following the liberation of the camp, those two weeks when, still living inside, I was able to see the camp from the exterior, the outside, from a new point of view, even though I was still living inside. And then, for example, there are the scenes from *Come Back Africa*, Rogosin's film on South Africa, behind which, as though the film were transparent, I kept seeing the quarantine camp, while on the screen were flashing pictures of the Negro suburbs of Johannesburg. There's also the panorama of the restricted zone in Madrid, that dusty, loathesome little valley, La Elipa, crammed with farm hands chased from their lands and situated a mere three hundred yards from luxury dwellings, that corner of earth filled with swarming flies and children's cries. It's an analogous world, and yet at the camp we had running water: we all know how devoted the S.S. were to hygiene, pedigreed dogs and Wagner's music.

That day, I had in fact tried to think of all that on my way back from the German village where we had gone to get a drink of pure water from the fountain. I had suddenly realized that this village was not the outside, it was simply another aspect, another inner aspect, of the society that had given birth to the German camps.

I was in front of the entrance to the camp, I was looking at the asphalt road leading to the S.S. quarters, to the factories and the Weimar road. It was from here that the Kommandos left for work, in the gray, rose-tinted light of dawn, or, in winter, in the light of the searchlights, to the lively military marches played by the camp orchestra. It

was by this road that we had arrived, in the middle of the
fifth night of that voyage with the guy from Semur. But
the guy from Semur had remained behind in the boxcar. It
was down this road that, just a day ago, we had marched
with our blank faces and our hatred of death, in pursuit of
the fleeing S.S., along the Weimar road. And when I leave,
I shall leave by this road. It was here that I witnessed the
arrival of the slow, staggering column of Polish Jews, in
the middle of that winter which has just ended, the day
when I had gone to talk with one of the Jehovah's Witnesses,
the time when they had asked me to prepare the escape of
Pierrot and two other pals.

That was the day I saw the Jewish children die.

Years have passed, sixteen years, and now that death is
already adolescent, it's reaching that serious age of the
postwar children, these post-voyage children. They are
sixteen years old, the age of that ancient, adolescent death.
And maybe I shall be able to tell about the death of the
Jewish children, describe that death in all its details, solely
in the hope—perhaps exaggerated, perhaps unrealizable—
that these children may hear it, or that even one of them
may hear it, were it only one of those children who is
reaching the solemnity of his sixteen years, the silence of
his sixteen years, their exigency. Perhaps, given that hope,
the time has come for me to tell the story of the Jewish
children, to tell of their death on this broad avenue of the
camp in the middle of the final winter of the war, that story
which has never been told, which has lain buried in my
memory like some mortal treasure, preying on it with a
sterile suffering. Perhaps it is out of pride that I have never
told anyone the story of the Jewish children, come from
Poland in the cold of the coldest winter of the war, come to
die on the broad avenue leading up to the camp entrance,
under the cheerless gaze of Hitler's eagles. Out of pride,
perhaps. As if that story did not concern everyone, especially

the children who are sixteen today, as if I had the right, or even the possibility, to keep it to myself any longer. It's true that I had decided to forget. At Eisenach, too, I had decided never to join the ranks of the official veterans. All right, I had forgotten, I had forgotten everything, from now on I can remember everything. I can tell the story of the Jewish children from Poland, not as a story that has happened to me especially, but above all one that happened to the Jewish children from Poland. That is, now, after these long years of willful oblivion, not only am I able to tell this story, I feel compelled to tell it. I have to speak out in the name of things that have happened, not in my own name. The story of the Jewish children in the name of the Jewish children. The story of their death on the broad avenue which led up to the camp entrance, beneath the stony gaze of the Nazi eagles, surrounded by the laughter of the S.S., in the name of death itself.

The Jewish children did not arrive in the middle of the night, as we had, but in the gray light of late afternoon.

It was the last winter of that war, the coldest winter of that war whose outcome had been decided in the cold and snow. The Germans had been driven from their positions by a mighty Soviet offensive that was sweeping across Poland, and whenever they had time they were evacuating the deportees that they had assembled in the Polish camps. For days, for weeks on end, in our camp not far from Weimar, in the beech forest above Weimar, we had seen these convoys of evacuated prisoners arriving. The trees were covered with snow, the roads were covered with snow, and in the quarantine camp you sank down into the snow up to your knees. The Jews from Poland were stacked into the freight cars almost two hundred to a car, and they had traveled for days and days with nothing to eat or drink, in the cold of that coldest winter of that war. When, at the train station of the camp, they opened the sliding doors, nothing stirred, most of the Jews had died standing up, died of cold, died of hunger, and they had to unload the cars as if they had transported wood, for example, and the bodies fell stiffly out onto the station platform, where they piled them up prior to taking them, in whole truckloads, directly to the crematorium. Yet there were some survivors, there were some Jews still alive, moribund in the midst of that pile of frozen corpses in the boxcars. One day, in one of the cars where there were some survivors, when they separated the pile of frozen bodies, which were often stuck together by their rigid, frozen clothing, they discovered a group of Jewish children. Suddenly, in the snow on the station platform, amid the snow-covered trees, there was a group of Jewish children, about fifteen in all, gazing about with an air of amazement, looking at the corpses piled up as the trunks of trees already stripped of their bark are piled along the sides of roads, waiting to be taken somewhere else, looking at the trees and the snow on the trees, looking like children do. And at first the S.S. seemed perturbed, as though they didn't know what to do with these children, who ranged in age from eight or so to twelve, although some of them, because they were so terribly thin and because of the expression in their eyes, looked like old men. But it seemed that the S.S., at least in the beginning, didn't know what to do with these children, and they gathered them in one corner, perhaps stalling for time while they sent for instructions, meanwhile escorting the few dozen surviving adults out of that particular convoy along the broad avenue. And some of these survivors will still have time to die before reaching the camp entrance, I remember seeing some of these survivors collapse on the way, as if their lives, only faintly burning in the welter of frozen bodies in the boxcars, suddenly went out altogether, some of them falling stiffly, straight from a standing position like trees struck by lightning, onto the dirty—and in places muddy—snow, in the midst of the immaculate snow on the tall, trembling beeches, others falling first to their knees, making an effort to get up, in order to drag themselves a few yards farther, then finally remaining stretched out, their arms above their heads, their fleshless hands clawing at the snow in what seemed to be one final effort to crawl a few inches closer to that gate over there, as if that gate marked the end of the snow, and winter and death. But finally there was nobody left on the station platform except the fifteen Jewish children. At that point the S.S. returned in full force, they must have received precise instructions, or else been given a free hand, perhaps they had been allowed to improvise the manner in which the children were to be murdered. Anyway, they returned in full force, with their dogs, and they were laughing boisterously, joking back and forth at the top of their lungs, which sent them into gales of laughter. They formed a semicircle and they shoved the fifteen children before them down the broad avenue. I remember, the kids kept looking around, they were looking at the S.S., at first they must have thought that they were merely being escorted to the camp, as they had seen their elders escorted earlier. But the S.S. loosed their dogs and began to hit the children with their clubs, to make them run, so that the hunt along the avenue could get under way, that hunt which they had made up or had been told to organize, and the Jewish children, urged on by the clubs, bullied by the dogs jumping around them, the well-trained dogs that snapped at their legs without barking or growling, the Jewish children began to run down the broad avenue toward the gate of the camp. Perhaps at that point they still had not understood what was in store for them, perhaps they thought that this was merely one last joke to be played on them before they were allowed to enter the camp. And the children were running, their large, long-vizored caps pulled down to their ears, and their legs were moving awkwardly, slowly and jerkily, as in the old silent films, as in nightmares when you run with all your might and can't move a step ahead and the thing pursuing you is going to overtake you, and it does overtake you and you awake in a cold sweat, and that thing, that pack of dogs and S.S., running behind the Jewish children, soon engulfed the weakest among them, the ones who were only eight years old, perhaps, the ones who no longer had the strength to move, who were knocked down, trampled on, clubbed on the ground, who lay there on the avenue, their skinny disjointed bodies marking the progress of that hunt, of that pack swarming over them. And soon there were only two left, one big and one small, both having lost their caps in their mad race, and their eyes were shining like splinters of ice in their gray faces, and the little one began to fall behind, the S.S. were howling behind them and then the dogs began to howl too, the smell of blood was driving them mad, and then the bigger of the two children slowed his pace to take the hand of the smaller, who was already stumbling, and together they covered a few more yards, the older one's right hand clasping the smaller one's left hand, running straight ahead till the blows of the clubs felled them and, together they dropped, their faces to the ground, their hands clasped for all eternity. The S.S. collected their dogs, who were growling, and walked back in the opposite direction, firing a bullet point-blank into the head of each of the children who had fallen on the broad avenue, beneath the empty gaze of the Hitlerian eagles.

But today the avenue is deserted in the April sun. Over there, at the intersection in front of the Totenkopf barracks, an American jeep is turning around.

I turn and walk toward the grilled gate.

I have to find Diego, or else Walter. I feel like talking with the boys. I show my pass to the American sentinel and glance up at the inscription, in large, wrought-iron letters,

set above the bars. ARBEIT MACHT FREI. Freedom
Through Work. It's a fine, paternalistic maxim, it's for our
own good that we've been imprisoned here, it's through
forced labor that they have taught us the meaning of freedom. It's a noble maxim, without a doubt, nor is it a proof
of cynical humor on the part of the S.S., it's merely that
the S.S. are convinced that they are right.

I've gone through the gate, and I wander aimlessly
through the streets of the camp, glancing left and right, on
the lookout for the boys.

Then, along the wide pathway that skirts the kitchens, at
the corner of Block 34, I see Emile. He's standing in the
sun, his arms dangling loosely at his sides, staring blankly
into space.

Not too long ago I thought of Emile, I remembered him
a few weeks ago, at the time of Alfredo's arrest. I was
wondering, at the time of Alfredo's arrest, why some people
hold out and others do not, why some people resist police
intimidation and torture and others do not. Alfredo had held
out, and during those days, as I was dwelling on the reasons why some people hold out and others do not, I remembered Emile. Even more serious, though, is the difficulty,
the quasi-impossibility, of establishing rational criteria for
the strength of some people and the weakness of others,
and this requires a good deal of thought. Anyway, I was
mulling this over in my mind, for the purely empirical observation that this person resisted and that one did not
wasn't really very reassuring. Alfredo: it was a Thursday,
we were supposed to meet at eleven o'clock. It was windy,
a dry, cutting wind sweeping down off the snowy peaks. I
waited for Alfredo for a quarter of an hour, those fifteen
extra minutes we allow before coming to the conclusion
that something has happened to him. The fifteen minutes
passed, something has happened to him. First you think of
some ordinary obstacle, some banal but unpredictable event.

You chase from your mind the idea that it might be something serious, really serious. But a dull anxiety begins to gnaw at your heart, a painful contraction of all the muscles inside. I lit a cigarette, I left, we held the meeting anyway. Later I called Alfredo from a public phone. A man's voice answered, it wasn't Alfredo's. Was it his father? I couldn't swear to it. The voice pressed me to give my name, to know who was calling Alfredo. The voice said that Alfredo was sick, why didn't I come by and see him, he'd be delighted to have the visit. I said: "Right you are, sir, very good. Thanks very much." Outside, I stood on the sidewalk thinking about that voice. It wasn't Alfredo's father, obviously. It was a trap, nothing but a blatant, good old-fashioned trap. I was smoking a cigarette, standing in the icy wind sweeping down from the snowy slopes and the cigarette had a bitter taste and I was thinking that we had to put into immediate effect all security measures, to try and cut every link between Alfredo and the organization. As for the rest, that depended on Alfredo, on whether or not he held out.

I was smoking my cigarette, and I was overwhelmed with the feeling that all this had happened before, with the bitter feeling of motions often made before that would have to be made again. It wasn't all that complicated, actually a routine job, a few phone calls to be made, several visits, that's all. Afterward, there was nothing to do but wait. In a few hours we would begin receiving some news, transmitted from several sources simultaneously, sometimes reaching us via the most unexpected, round-about routes. The night watchman was reported to have seen Alfredo leaving in handcuffs at three in the morning, surrounded by police. At dawn, he apparently passed on the information to the baker who has a shop six doors away, and this baker happens to be connected with one of our neighborhood units. In a few hours telephones will start ringing and odd-sounding sentences spoken: "Hello, Robert asked me to call you to say that your order will be delivered at two o'clock," which means that the person called is supposed to report to a specified place, to be apprised of an important piece of news. In a few hours, we will have created around Alfredo a zone of silence, of closed doors, of unexpected absences, of packages moved and papers put into safekeeping, of women waiting once again, as they have often waited during the past twenty years, more than twenty years. In a few hours, we shall weave the tightest network of solitary gestures, of thoughts confronting—each for himself, in the silence of himself—the torture of this friend and colleague which, tomorrow, may be our own torture. We'll have some news, some idea of how Alfredo's arrest came about and what it means, we may be able to deduce whether it's linked to some large-scale operation. And, finally, we'll have enough concrete information to work on so that we can take steps to counter any blows.

There was nothing to do but wait. It was the end of autumn, sixteen years after that other autumn at Auxerre. I remember, there were roses in the garden of the Gestapo. I tossed away one cigarette, lighted another and thought of Alfredo. I was thinking that he was going to hold out, not only because the tortures employed are no longer what they used to be. I was thinking that he would have held out anyway, even in the old days, or that he would have died on the rack. That was what I was thinking, and I was trying to grasp the rational elements of that thought, the fixed points on which that spontaneous conviction rested. When you think about it, it's frightening to realize that for years we've been constantly compelled to scan our colleagues faces, to be watchful for any possible break in their voices, anything unusual in their gestures in a certain circumstance, or in the way they react to a certain situation, to try and get some idea of how, if it should ever happen, they would stand up under torture. But it's a practical problem that has to be considered, absolutely, it would be criminal not to. It's frightening to think that torture is a practical problem, that the capacity to stand up under torture has to be considered practically. Yet it's a fact, we didn't choose it, but we're none the less obliged to take it into account. A man ought to be able to be a man even if he's incapable of resisting torture, and yet, things being what they are, a man ceases to be the man he was, that he might become, the moment he yields under torture and denounces his comrades. Things being what they are, the possibility of being a man is bound to the possibility of torture, to the possibility of yielding to torture.

I took several taxis, went where I had to go, did what I had to do, what anyone could do, and I kept on waiting, continuing the routine gestures of daily life, but waiting with all my might. Alfredo had to hold out, if he didn't we would all be weakened by it. Alfredo had to hold out, so that all of us would be strengthened by his victory. I was thinking of all that, and I knew that Alfredo, as they hit and clubbed him, was thinking of it too. At this minute he's thinking that his silence is not only a personal victory, it's a victory that we shall all share with him. He knows that our truth will don the shining armor of his silence, and that helps him smile in his silence.

Hours went by, nothing happened, it was Alfredo's silence that made this calm possible. They haven't rung at anyone's door at three in the morning, that dreaded hour when the searches and initial knocks catch you cold, your mouth filled with sleep. It is Alfredo's silence which allows the men in the threatened houses to sleep. Hours went by, nothing happened, once again we're going to emerge victorious. I remember that spring day eight months ago, I was seated on the bench with Alfredo and Eduardo. It was warm, we were in the sun, the gently rolling lawns stretched in front of us. We were exchanging small talk, and I don't remember how the conversation got onto *The Question*. It's a book that we had read carefully, that we had re-read, because it's much more than a document. For us it's a book of practical importance, full of information. A work tool, in a way. For it is extremely useful to understand, with such clarity, such absolute authority, with no words wasted, that one can stand up under electric shocks, that, in spite of truth serum, one can refrain from talking. We discussed *The Question* from a practical point of view, quite calmly, for us it's a practical book. It was a beautiful book, a useful book, which helped us to live. Maybe Alfredo also remembered that conversation in the sunny park overlooking the blue mountains still covered with a few traces of snow, overlooking the harsh landscape of oak and olive trees. Afterward, we had a beer together before breaking up. It was cool. It was a good feeling to be thirsty and to quench your thirst.

Those days just a few weeks ago, I remembered Emile. The last time I saw him, he was standing in the sunlight at the corner of Block 34, his arms dangling at his sides. I walked right past him, I turned my head away, I didn't have the courage to face his lifeless stare, his despair, yes, certainly, his everlasting despair, on this spring day which for him was not the start of a new life, but the end, yes, the end of a whole life. Emile had held out, for twelve years he had held out and suddenly, a month ago, when the battle was already won and we could feel the freedom that was fast approaching, the whole spring was filled with sounds and suggestions of that approaching freedom, a month ago he gave up. He gave up in the most stupid, the most cowardly fashion, you might even say he gave up gratuitously. When the S.S., who were desperate, who had reached the end of their rope, had called for volunteers for the German Army a month before and not received a single response from all the thousands of political prisoners, they had threatened the section chiefs. Then, next to the names of a few common law criminals who had volunteered, Emile had written in the name of a deportee in his section, an Alsatian mobilized by force into the Wehrmacht, who had deserted and been imprisoned as a deserter. He had volunteered his name without telling him, of course, in his capacity of section chief. He had sent this Alsatian to his death, or to the depths of despair, he had made of this young Alsatian a man forever lost, even if he were to survive, a man who would no longer have confidence in anything, a man henceforth stripped of all human hope. I had seen this Alsatian cry the day the S.S. came for him, since he was on the list of volunteers. We stood around him, we didn't know what to say to him, he was crying, rejected, he didn't understand what was happening to him, he didn't understand anything any more, he was a lost soul.

Emile was chief of the section, we were proud of his quiet calm, his generosity, we were happy to see him emerging from these twelve years of horror with a quiet smile in his blue eyes, his face hollowed, ravaged by the horrors of these twelve years. And now, suddenly, he left us, he collapsed into the night of these past twelve years, now he became one of the living examples of this horror, this interminable twelve-year-long night. Now, just when the S.S. were beaten, Emile became a living example of their victory, that is, of our past, already dying defeat, but carrying with it as it died Emile's living corpse.

He was there, at the corner of Block 34, in the sunlight, his arms dangling. I turned my head away. He was no longer with us. He, like the woman a while ago, like her dead sons, like the two dead sons of that woman in her house overlooking the crematorium, was on the side of death, which was of the past but still present. As for us, we had to start learning how to live.

"I suppose," says the guy from Semur, "I suppose that in any case they'll put us on hard labor."

We're there trying to guess what kind of work the S.S. are going to provide us with in the camp where we're headed.

"Say, friend," says a voice somewhere behind us.

The guy from Semur looks around.

"You talking to us?" he asks.

"Yes," the voice says, "to your pal. I want to ask him something."

But I'm caught in the mass of bodies. I can't turn around toward the voice of this person who wants to ask me something.

"Go ahead," I say to him, stretching my head as far as I can. "Go ahead, I'm listening."

I can hear the man's voice at my back, and the guy from Semur is looking at him as he talks.

"That motorcycle you were talking about," the voice says, "did you drive it to the Taboo maquis?"

"Yes," I answer, "you know it?"

"To the Taboo just above Larrey?" the voice says.

"That's the one. Why, do you know it?"

"I was there," the voice says.

"Really, when was that?"

"I've practically just come from there," the voice says. "The S.S. mopped up the region a month ago. There isn't any Taboo any more."

I feel as though someone has hit me. Obviously, the war goes on, things never remain immutable, the way they were when I was arrested. But knowing the S.S. has liquidated the Taboo is a terrible blow.

"Shit," I say. Which is exactly what I think.

"I remember that motorcycle," the voice says. "We used it after you left."

"It was a good motorcycle. Almost new."

I remember that excursion on the autumn roads, and it really pisses me off that they've liquidated the Taboo.

"If you're really the guy with the motorcycle—" the voice begins.

"I'm the one, sure I'm the one," I break in.

"Yes, sure you are," the voice says. "It was just the way I put it. What I meant to say was, since it's you, you made another trip to the Taboo unit."

"That's right," I say, "in a Citroën. We had some weapons for you."

"That's right," the voice says. "I remember that time too. You had a revolver with a long barrel painted red, and we all wanted one just like it."

"Right you are," I say with a laugh, "that was a real cannon."

"That time you were with another guy," says the voice. "A tall guy with glasses."

The tall guy with glasses was Hans.

"That's right," I say.

"He was with us when the battle began," the voice says.

"What battle?" I say, suddenly concerned.

"When the S.S. launched their attack, the tall fellow with glasses was with us."

"Why? Why had he come back?"

"I don't know, pal," says the voice of the guy who was in the Taboo unit. "He'd come back, that's all I know."

"So what happened?"

"I don't know," the voice says. "The battle went on for

half a day—the evening and part of the night—right there, on both sides of the road. Then we began to fall back toward the interior, in order to disperse."

"And my pal?"

"I don't know about your pal. He stayed behind with the covering group," the voice says.

Hans had remained behind with the covering group.

"You didn't see him again?" I ask.

"No," the voice says. "After we dispersed I was caught in a roadblock at Chatillon. We didn't see any of the guys from the covering group."

Hans had stayed behind with the covering group, as I might have predicted.

Later, during the second half of May, two years from now, the year of my return, Michel and I visited all the farms in the area, from Laignes to Chatillon, from Semur to Larrey, searching for some trace of Hans. Michel was in the First Army, and just after the surrender of Germany he had received a pass. We had searched for some trace of Hans, but there wasn't any trace of Hans. It was in the spring, Michel had pulled some strings and secured a car and we drove to Joigny on some official mission. Irène had not returned to Joigny. She had died in Bergen-Belsen, of typhus, a few days after the arrival of the English troops. Her mother fed us in the kitchen we had known in the past, and in the cellar the persistent odor of plastic still lingered. She showed us a clipping from a local paper relating Irène's death in Bergen-Belsen. Albert had been shot. Olivier had died at Dora. Julien was dead too, they had taken him by surprise at Laroche, he had put up a great fight and saved his last bullet for himself. I remember he used to say: "Torture, thanks a lot, if I have anything to say about it I'll blow out my brains." He had blown out his brains. Michel and I listened to Irène's mother, we listened to her faltering voice. We ate stewed rabbit with a mustard sauce, we didn't say a word, and the shadows of our dead comrades were all around us.

A week later, we managed to find one of the survivors of the Taboo. It was on a farm not far from Laignes, we waited in the courtyard of the farm for the men to return from the fields. We waited with the farmer's wife, it was her son who had survived the massacre of the Taboo. In a slow but clear voice she told us the long story of those long years. We were only half-listening, because we knew the story. That wasn't the story we were interested in now, it was Hans, the trace of Hans, the memory of Hans. The farmer's wife told us that long story, and from time to time she would break in to say: "How about a glass of white wine?" and she would look at us and add: "Or a little cider?" But she didn't give us any time to say that, yes, we'd be happy to have a glass of white wine, she went right on with that long story of the long years that had just come to an end.

Yesterday, in a bistro near Semur, where we were having some bread and cheese and ham, accompanied by a local white wine that was really out of this world, Michel had said, after a prolonged silence between us:

"You know, you haven't told me anything yet."

I know what he's referring to, but I don't want to know. The bread, the ham, the cheese, the local wine: these are things you have to learn to enjoy again. You have to work at it. I don't feel like telling anything.

"Tell?" I reply, "what is there to tell?"

Michel looks at me.

"That's just it," he says, "I don't know."

I cut a small square of bread, cut a small square of cheese, I put the bread beneath the cheese, and I eat it. Then a swallow of local wine.

"Frankly, I don't know what there would be to tell."

Michel is eating too. Then he says:

"Maybe too many things?"

"Or not enough, not enough compared to what can never be told."

This time Michel seems surprised.

"Are you sure?"

"No," I have to admit, "maybe it was only an empty phrase."

"That's my feeling."

"Anyway," I add, "I need time."

Michel thinks about that.

"Time to forget maybe," he says. "So that you can tell after you've forgotten."

"That's it, more or less."

And we never raised the subject again, neither during the days that followed, while we were searching for some trace of Hans, nor even later. And now that the time of forgetfulness has come, that is, now that this past surges back into my memory more strongly than ever, I still can't tell Michel. Now I don't know where to find him.

The next day we were in the courtyard of that farm, and the mother of the boy who had survived the Taboo massacre was telling us the long story of those long years. Then the men came back. The men escorted us into the long common room of the farmhouse, and at long last we got to taste that white wine.

The long common room—or maybe it was the kitchen— was cool and warm, that is warm, but with a kind of cool draft running through it, unless it was me shivering, shivers running up and down my spine, fatigue maybe, or perhaps it was the recollection of the Taboo massacre that this fellow was relating without any trace of emotion, no doubt being incapable of highlighting or emphasizing the most important episodes, but for that very reason the effect on us was all the more marked, Michel felt it too, I think, at least I had that impression, although we never discussed it

again later, when we drove away. Chaos and night, chaos
and death, and Hans had remained behind in the covering
group, the fellow remembered it perfectly well, that is, he
hadn't remained, he had decided to stay, he had chosen it.
Michel surely remembers—he was the one who told me
about it—that conversation with Hans, he had shown me
the place, the spot where it had occurred, and Hans saying
to him: "I don't want to die a Jew's death," and Michel
asking him, "What do you mean by that?" and that meant,
"I don't want to die merely because I'm a Jew," he refused
to have his destiny inscribed in his body. Michel said—he
said it to me—that Hans had used much cruder, more
graphic terms than that, and that didn't surprise me, Hans
was in the habit of concealing, beneath a surface of verbal
extravagance, his deepest feelings, since that's the way people classify real feelings, as if feelings had varying densities,
some of them floating, but on what water, the others trail-
ing in the depths, in what sludge of the substrata. The fact
is that Hans didn't want to die, insofar as he had to die,
merely because he was Jewish; he thought, and I think, from
what he had said to Michel about it and what Michel reported to me, that that wasn't a good, or perhaps valid,
enough reason, not a sufficiently valid reason to die, he
thought, certainly, that one had to have other reasons for
dying, that is, for being killed, because—and this I'm sure
of—he had no desire to die, simply the need to give the
Germans other reasons to kill him, if he had to be killed,
than the mere fact of his being Jewish. After that we had
a second glass of wine, and then a third, and then we sat
down to eat, for "surely you'll stay and have something
to eat with us," and the guy was still spinning his dull
story, his hallucinating, dull and disordered story of the
Taboo massacre, which had been something dull and dis-
organized, not any brilliant battle, something dull and
gray in the winter up on the high slopes, among the winter

trees, a kind of police, or pinpointing, operation, in that forest from which, night after night, the maquis swept down onto all the roads and villages of the region. Once or twice, I don't remember how many times, I had participated in these nocturnal raids, in that souped-up Citroën, or maybe I'm confusing it with another resistance unit, I don't believe so though, and throughout the night the roads were ours, yes, all night long, the villages were ours, night after night.

The fact is Hans had remained behind in the covering group.

"Your pal, the tall guy with glasses," says the guy from the farm, "Philippe we called him, as I remember, he was the one who finally took over the automatic rifle."

The farmer's wife is seeing to it we have enough to eat, she's standing with both hands resting on the back of a chair, watching her son, and her look is an April rain shot through with sunlight, shining drops of pure joy, a sudden shower pouring down upon the lowered, pensive, slowly chewing face of her son who's harking back to the memory of that massacre from which he emerged safe and sound, ah yes, her son safe and sound beside her, alive, taciturn or gay, grumbling, "Ma, I'm hungry, Ma, I'm thirsty, Ma, give me something to drink."

"You're not eating, mother?" her husband asks.

Thus that story began to take shape, but there was always a point at which Hans suddenly disappeared. That man in the train, that anonymous voice in the semi-darkness of the boxcar, with whom it had all begun, spoke of Hans with considerable precision up to the point where the rout had begun. And this guy, the son of these farmers who lived not far from Laignes, took up the thread, providing further details about the same facts, another facet of the facts which carried the story further along, since he had remained behind with Hans a while longer, this farmer's son belonged to a group of young peasants of the region who had not fallen back, who had not tried to break through the German encirclement but had, on the contrary, drawing on their knowledge of every path, every sunken road, every hedge, copse, clearing, slope, every embankment, tilled field and pasture, had slipped through the German lines, crawling at one point between the S.S. sentinels, and some of them had succeeded in reaching friendly farms in the vicinity, doors opening in the night to let them in, the whole family standing in the dark behind closed shutters, listening breathlessly to the sound of the S.S. machine guns in the night, up on the Taboo heights.

And this tale told by the guy from Laignes, the son of these Laignes farmers, reminded me of another, that is, to be more exact, while this guy is wheeling off his story, stumbling over his sentences as he had that night stumbled over the roots and stones and through the brambles, another night march comes to mind, that is, the thought that I ought to be thinking of another march in the night, evoked by the one I'm hearing, but still not clear, without my knowing yet what that other march in the night was or who was making it, prowls at the edges of my memory, simmers softly somewhere beneath this story and the thoughts this story stirs up. But the fact is that there comes a point in this story where Hans disappears. And suddenly I realize that we'll never discover any trace of Hans.

Bloch, on the other hand, accepted the fact he was a Jew. It terrified him, of course, his lips were ghastly pale and he was shaking when I met him halfway down the rue Soufflot and together we walked toward the Henri IV Lycée. But he accepted it, that is, he settled into it straight away, with resignation (and perhaps even with a joyful resignation, though I can't swear to it, with a certain kind of joy in resigning himself, in accepting the fact that he was a Jew, an ignominious condition today, a condition involving risks, but these risks, he must have told himself with that certain sorrowful joy, had always been part of being Jewish: yesterday inwardly different from the others, today—the yellow star of David—made manifest), with terror and joy, with a certain pride, why not, a corrosive, acid, self-destructive pride.

"It would be better for you not to be seen with me," he says halfway up the rue Soufflot, on our way to our philosophy class that morning.

"Why?" I ask, although I know why. But I want him to say why.

"You know very well," he says. He jerks his chin toward the yellow star sewed onto his gray overcoat.

At that I laugh, and I'm afraid that in my laugh—and if there was I really want to apologize for it—I'm afraid there was a trace of contempt, maybe not contempt exactly, but something superior, something chilling that could have hurt Bloch's pride, that sad pride which finally—for the worse, not for the better, only for the worse—finally burst into the open, that monstrous truth of his being different from us.

"So what?" I tell him. "You don't think I'm going to play their little game."

"What game?" he says, and, keeping step, we continue walking together.

"Maybe game's not the right word," I say. "Their effort, their decision to isolate you, make you an outsider."

"But it's true," he says, and he smiles, and that's when I thought I detected that trace of sad, corrosive pride in his smile.

"That's your own business," I tell him, "whether or not to accept it. But for me my business—and there's nothing you can do to change it—is to ignore it. That you can't do anything about, it's my business."

He shakes his head and says nothing more and we reach

the school just as the bell is ringing and we dash toward philosophy class, Bertrand is going to explain to us once again why and how the mind is its own creator, and once again I'm going to pretend I believe that phantasmagoria.

It was the following day, in any event not long after Bloch had arrived with his yellow star—and our philosophy class consisted entirely of good solid Frenchmen, there was only that single, solitary yellow star, Bloch's, all the more striking (as for me, it was only later on that things fell into place, and I wore not a yellow star but a red triangle pointing downward to the heart, my red triangle signifying Spanish Red, with an "S" above it)—so it was the following day, or two days later, that the mathematics teacher felt obliged to make a few remarks about that yellow star, about Jews in general, about the way the world was evolving. Bloch had glanced over at me, he was smiling as he had the other day, he was putting up a bold front, this was only the first stage of that long sacrifice his life was henceforth to be, it was all written in the texts, he was smiling, no doubt already thinking of the sacrifices yet to come, the sacrifices also written, also described, already engraved.

But neither Bloch nor I nor anyone else had thought of Le Cloarec, we had forgotten that somewhere there is always a son of Brittany ready to stir up a little trouble. Le Cloarec had promptly taken charge of the situation. At the beginning of the course in November, we went to the Arc de Triomphe together, after having agreed—laughing and slapping each other on the back—on the following points: first, that we all shat upon World War I, we said to hell with it, to hell with the tombs of the unknown soldiers, not the unknown soldiers themselves, the tombs that are raised to them after they have been butchered anonymously; that was the point of departure, Le Cloarec said, the abstract intentional reference of our act, he added, and to that I added (whence the laughs and back-slapping) that it was the horizon on which was revealed the final consistence, the con-sis-tent finality of our project, toward which our pro-ject ec-stat-ically unfolded. But meanwhile, said Le Cloarec, let's stick to reality, let's come back to reality, and I, let us throw ourselves, let us *geworf* ourselves into the disordered utensibility of the concrete world, that is, we damn and condemn the imperialist war, ergo the imperialists, and among them we especially damn and condemn the especially aggressive, virulent and truimphant imperialists, the Nazis; therefore, in practical terms, we're going to take part in a demonstration at the tomb of the unknown soldier, I the Breton and you the alien, the damn dirty Spanish Red, because today, concretely, that is what can annoy the Nazis the most, the Nazis and all their dear little ensconced friends. I mean the ones who have erected this tomb to the unknown soldier; and there it was, the circle was closed, methodically and dialectically, hence the hearty back-slapping. In any case, we would have gone to that march on the Etoile, all this was merely for our own benefit, we would have marched with hundreds of other students (I didn't think there would be so many of us), beneath the gray November sky, we would have broken through that line of French police at the level of the rue Marbeuf (Le Cloarec was a natural phenomenon), and we would have seen that column of combat-ready German soldiers emerging from the Avenue Georges V, that mechanical, gutteral sound of the boots, the arms, and the commandants' voice; and still we would have pushed on to the Etoile, since that was what had to be done.

So Le Cloarec promptly took charge of the affair.

When he outlined his plan, I said to him: "You see, that little bretonized, bretonish, breton-like head of a Breton still contains a few ideas." Which made him laugh. And which made the others shout in unison "West-State" in stentorian tones, and that made the Corsican's head, the head of the Corsican pimp, the Corsican cop, the head supervisor, turn in our direction. But it was during recess, we were outside in the school yard, there was nothing he could say. I was the one who had made up that joke, which greatly amused Le Cloarec, I had told the others that his father knew only two words of French and that during World War I, whenever he stormed the German trenches he would shout these two words with all his heart and soul, these two words which for his father summed up the full grandeur of France, the Cartesian mind, the victories of '89, these two words which he had learned to read on the freight cars of the railroad serving Brittany. And ever since, they would laugh and shout in unison "West-State" each time Le Cloarec stirred up a little trouble, which he was fairly prone to do. But when I told them that I hadn't made anything up, that the story could be found in Claudel, in *Conversations in the Loir-et-Cher,* a book by the illustrious French ambassador. I really think they didn't want to believe me. "You're being farcical," Le Cloarec used to say to me. "You've got it in for our national glories," said Raoul. It was in vain that I insisted, that I told them that Claudel relates the whole thing with great gravity, with tears between the lines, reveling in that "West-State" bit, they didn't want to believe me. They didn't even dream of verifying what I said, they had decided that my attributing such a stupidity to Claudel was an act of pure perversity on my part.

So, as I said, Le Cloarec took charge of the affair. They had all decided to take part in the Breton's march. "West-State," that great Druid-like cry, had become the byword, the slogan, whispered or shouted, of the action being prepared. Everybody except Pinel, of course. Pinel was the model student in all its horror, always in the top three of his class no matter what the subject, as if it were possible to be in the top three everywhere without fooling oneself, without stupidly forcing oneself to be interested in courses that are really of no interest. Pinel had said that he was not taking part in the march, he was appalled at the idea, from that moment on his name was mud, and we did our best to make life impossible for him. So for the next mathematics course, when Rablon came into the classroom without glancing at anyone (for he was short and waited till he was on the dais before looking daggers at us), all of us, except Pinel, had sewed a yellow star on our chests, with the three letters JEW stitched in black on the yellow background of the star. Bloch, I must say, was terribly upset and was muttering in a voice so low you could barely hear him that we were all crazy, that it was mad, and Pinel was standing very straight, puffing out his chest to show that he wasn't wearing the yellow star. As always, Rablon, once he was up on the dais, Rablon-the-mathematics-man, looked daggers at this class of would-be philosophers, of problem students (Philosophy II was traditionally a mixture of students who wrote good term papers and others who were unruly: I don't know whether the tradition still exists at the Henry IV Lycée), and suddenly his gaze froze, his eyes grew glassy, his mouth sagged, all I could see was his adam's apple bouncing up and down in a sort of spasmodic movement, Rablon, caught short, taken completely aback by this staggering uppercut to his creepy face, that sea of yellow stars unfurling toward him, spreading like a wave just before it breaks, rising as the tiers of the classroom rose, Rablon opened his mouth, I could have sworn he was going to start screaming, but his mouth remained open and nothing came out, and his adam's apple bobbed spasmodically up and down in his skinny neck. He remained like that for an eternity, and it was so quiet in the classroom you could have heard a pin drop, and finally Rablon had an unexpected reaction, he turned to Pinel and in a snarling, scathing, despondent voice began calling Pinel every name in the book. Pinel couldn't believe his ears. "You always want to stand out, Pinel," he said to him, "you never want to do what the others do," and he directed the fire of all his questions at Pinel, he made him recite the whole cosmography, all the mathematics learned to date (yes, Pinel had learned it all), since the start of the year. And when the hour was over, he left without saying a word and we saluted Le Cloarec's victory, our victory, with an unanimous cry of "West-State," and we added a "Pinel to the gallows" for good measure.

"No, no," I say, "he was German."

The farmer looks at me as though I were speaking Greek. His son, the guy who had survived the Taboo massacre, is also looking at me. His mother isn't there, she's gone to fetch something.

"What's that?" the farmer says.

At one point, when he had interrupted his son's tale to offer a few general remarks on life and people, he had said that as long as there were Frenchmen like him, like our friend Philippe, France would never be lost.

"He was German," I say. "He wasn't French, he was German."

Michel looks at me wearily, he must be thinking that here I go again annoying the hell out of people with my habit of clarifying everything, of dotting my i's and crossing my t's.

"And he was Jewish to boot," I say. "A German Jew."

Wearily, Michel explains in somewhat clearer terms that the Philippe in question was Hans, why Hans was Philippe. That gives them pause, obviously, they shake their heads, that impresses them, no question about it. He was a German Jew, I'm thinking, and he didn't want to die like a Jew, and the fact is that now we don't know how he did die. I saw plenty of other Jews die, saw them die like Jews, or rather solely because they were Jews, as if they considered that being Jewish was sufficient reason to die this way, to let themselves be murdered.

But it so happened that we didn't know how Hans had died. There was simply a point in the story, in the tale of this massacre of the Taboo, when Hans always disappeared, no matter who was telling it.

The next day (perhaps) we trampled down the grass growing among the tall trees of that forest which had been the Taboo, and it was here, on this spot, that Hans had disappeared. Michel is walking on ahead, striking the stems of the tall grass with the end of a flexible stick. I stop for a moment and listen to the forest. We ought to pause more often, take more time to listen to the forest. Whole centuries of my life have gone by without my being able to listen to the forest. I stop and listen. That dull paralyzing joy takes root in the certainty of the absolute contingency of my presence here, of my radical uselessness. I'm not necessary for this rustling forest to exist, therein lies the source of that muted joy. Michel wanders off among the trees, and it was here that Hans disappeared. In the end, it was he who had taken over the machine gun, according to what the guy from the farm had said yesterday (the day before yesterday, who knows). Hans didn't have time to listen to the forest, all he could hear during that winter night of the Taboo massacre was the dry, chaotic staccato of gunfire around him. He remained there alone, in the end, glued to his machine gun, profoundly pleased, I imagine, to be stealing a death steeped in resignation from the S.S., pleased to be inflicting death upon them, violent and dangerous, murdering the murderers, on that blind, chaotic night when the Taboo massacre took place.

Michel retraces his steps and calls out:

"What are you doing?"

"I'm listening."

"Listening to what?"

"Simply listening."

Michel stops mowing the tall grass and listens too.

"So what do you hear?" he says after a while.

"Nothing."

I walk over to where he's standing with his arm out straight, holding the supple stick with which he's been cutting the stems of the tall grass. I offer him a cigarette. We both smoke in silence.

"Where was the camp, do you remember?" Michel asks.

"Over there," I say, "to the right."

We set off walking again. Now the forest is silent. The sound of our footsteps has reduced the forest to silence.

"Was it you who told me a story about a night march in the forest, a long march in the forest that went on night after night?" I ask Michel.

He glances at me, then looks around. We're walking in the forest, but it's daylight, it's spring.

"I don't know what you're talking about," Michel says. "No, I don't remember any walk in the forest at night that I might have mentioned to you."

With broad, well-aimed movements, he begins cutting the tall grass again. I have a strong feeling he's going to get on my nerves if he keeps it up, that I'm soon going to be fed up with this gesture, mechanically repeated a thousand times.

"What's this story of a march all about?" he asks.

"Ever since that fellow at the farm told us about their flight through the forest the night of the Taboo, I have the feeling I'm about to remember another march by night in the forest. Another story, from somewhere else, but I can't quite place it."

"That sometimes happens," Michel says. And he starts mowing the grass again.

But we emerge into the clearing where the camp was, and I don't have a chance to tell him that he's beginning to get on my nerves.

The huts, I recall, were half underground. The boys had hollowed out a good-sized pit in the ground and shored up the walls with boards. No more than three feet of boards and thatch were above the level of the ground. There were three of these huts set on three apexes of a possible triangle, each of which was big enough to house at least ten men. Farther away, at the edge of the clearing, they had built a kind of garage for both the 402 Peugeot sedan and the small truck. The fuel drums were also over on that side of the clearing, covered with canvas and a network of branches; the whole thing must have gone up in flames the night of the Taboo. In the streams, and among the half-charred trees, we can still see some reddish and gray metal strips. From the spot where the huts had been we walk over to the center of the clearing. But the forest is fast effacing all trace of that life now three years old, of that already ancient death. Beneath the mounds of earth that have already been sifted through, we can still make out some pieces of wood and scrap metal. But everything is losing its human aspect, its appearance of objects made by man for human needs. The boards are reverting to wood, to rotten wood of course, dead wood, that much you can see, wood once again escaping from the destiny of men, being reintegrated into the cycle of the seasons, into the cycle of vegetative life and death. It takes a close look to make out the form of a tin can, the moving part of a Sten gun. That scrap metal is returning to the mineral world, to the process of exchange with the earth in which it is buried. The forest is effacing all trace of that former life, of that already old, already obsolete death of the Taboo. We're there, poking with our feet, for no apparent reason, stirring up with our feet the vestiges of this past that the tall grass is effacing, that the ferns are strangling in their multiple, trembling arms.

I was saying, only a few weeks ago I was saying to myself that I would like to see that: the grass and the bushes, the roots and brambles encroaching as the seasons go by, beneath the persistent Ettersberg rains, the winter snow, beneath the brief, rustling April sun, endlessly, obstinately encroaching, with that excessive obstinacy of natural things, among the cracks in the disjoined wood and the powdery crumbling of the cement that would split and yield to the thrust of the beech forest, unceasingly encroaching on this human countryside on the flank of the hill, this camp constructed by men, the grass and the roots repossessing the place where the camp had stood. The first to collapse would be the wooden barracks, those of the main camp, painted a pretty green, blending in easily, soon drowned by the invading tide of grass and shrubs, then later the two-story cement buildings, and then at last, surely long after all the other buildings, years later, remaining standing the longest, like the remembrance, or rather the evidence, the special symbol of that whole, the massive square chimney of the crematorium, till the day when the roots and brambles shall also overcome that tenacious resistance of brick and stone, that obstinate resistance of death rising among the waves of green covering over what was an extermination camp, and those shadows of dense black smoke, shot through with yellow, that perhaps still linger over this countryside, that smell of burning flesh still hovering over this countryside, when all the survivors, all of us, have long since disappeared, when there will no longer be any real memory of this, only the memory of memories related by those who will never really know (as one knows the acidity of a lemon, the feel of wool, the softness of a shoulder) what all this really was.

"Well," says Michel, "there's nothing more to see here."

And we left the clearing from the side where the guys had built a primitive road for the cars, a road linked to the forest trail which joined the road a few hundred yards below. We're on this forest trail, and Michel stops again.

"I wonder whether the sentinels were at their posts that day," he says with a frown.

"What do you mean?"

I look at Michel, failing to understand what difference a detail like that can make now.

"Yes, you remember," he says, "that time we surprised them in the clearing, on purpose, as a test, the sentinels weren't at their posts."

Yes, I remember, we caught them unawares, any stray Feld patrol could have done the same. We had a violent argument about it with the guys of the Taboo.

"But what does it matter now?" I ask.

"Still," Michel says, "I'm sure they were taken by surprise."

"You're beginning to have a military mind. Not bad, for a triple square."

He looks at me and smiles.

"You're right," he says. "Forget it."

"Anyway," I add, "if the S.S. came out in force they must have been forewarned, sentinels or no sentinels."

"Yes," Michel says, shaking his head. "Shall we go back to the farm now?"

"Of course, Captain, please come in, Captain," the farmer says.

He motions for us to come in, but before following the captain inside I turn around and look back. The farm stands about two hundred yards from the edge of the woods, overlooking a good stretch of the road winding up to the Taboo. They must have seen the S.S. trucks arriving, I wonder if they had time to warn the men. They must have, if they had time to, these farmers were on the best of terms with the boys from the Taboo.

I too go inside, Michel is already having a drink, it's impossible to refuse.

"Did you have time," I ask, after I too had a glass of brandy in my hand, "did you have time to warn the boys?"

The farmer shakes his head and turns to call back toward the interior of the house.

"Jeanine," he shouts.

He nods his head and explains to us. Yes, they did have time, it was his daughter who ran up to warn them.

"Were the sentinels at their posts?" Michel asks.

I feel like saying that the question doesn't have a god-damn thing to do with it, that this concern about the senti-nels is a sign of premature senility, but the farmer looks perplexed, he seems to be taking the question quite seri-ously, it's almost as though he felt he was to blame for not being able to give the right answer to that ridiculous question.

"I fully understand, Captain," he says, "we'll have to ask Jeanine if she remembers that detail."

But he quickly compensates for it.

"I mean, it's an important question.... The sentinels, Captain, I fully understand, the sentinels.... "

And he goes on shaking his head for a long time before emptying his glass with a sudden backward tilt of his whole body.

Jeanine, and then Jeanine's mother, and then the wife of the farm hand: the Germans finally stopped bothering them. They took away the men and the cattle. Her son was the unlucky one, they deported him to Germany.

"It can't be much longer before he comes home," the farmer says haltingly. "They're coming home every day now, the papers are full of it."

Michel glances at me, I glance at the farmer, the farmer is staring into space. There's a moment of silence.

"Have you heard from him since he was sent to Germany?" Michel asks finally.

"His mother has had two letters," the farmer says, "before the Allied landing. Nothing since. They even made him write in German. I wonder how the poor kid managed it."

"A friend probably wrote it for him," I say, "there are always some guys who know German and who help those who don't. It's the least they can do."

The farmers shakes his head and pours another round.

"What camp was your son in?" Michel asks.

"Buckenval," the farmer says.

I wonder why he pronounces it that way, but the fact is that most people do.

I can feel that Michel is starting to make a sign in my direction, so I look blank, freeze the muscles of my face, become dull, spongy, unavailable. I don't want to talk about the camps to this farmer whose son hasn't yet come back. If he were to learn that I had just returned, my presence here would lessen the chances of his son's survival, lessen his chances of seeing him come back alive. Each returning deportee who isn't his son reduces the chances that his son has survived, that he'll see him return alive. My own life, having already returned, increases the possibilities of his son's death. I hope Michel will understand this, that he won't pursue it any further.

But a door behind us opens and Jeanine comes in.

"Yes," Jeanine says, "I remember your friend very well."

We're walking again in the forest, toward the Taboo clearing.

"How old were you then?" I ask.

"Sixteen," Jeanine says.

We ate at the farm, we heard another account of the

Taboo massacre, another different account from another point of view, but it was identical all the same, the confusion, the night, the confused sounds of battle and, finally, the silence, the deep silence of winter on the heights of the Taboo. It's obvious that the farmer's wife, distraught and consumed by the wait, is living only for her son's return.

Michel remained behind at the farm, to putter over the motor of the car, he said. I'm walking again through the high grass toward the clearing of the Taboo, with Jeanine, who was sixteen at the time and remembers my pal very well.

"During the last days just before the battle," Jeanine says, "he sometimes came down to the farm."

Actually, the whole affair lasted a few hours, but for her, certainly, these few hours of confused sounds, the gunfire, the cries of the S.S. invading the farm, all that condenses and symbolizes, finally, the reality of those five long years of war, her whole adolescence. It was a battle that symbolizes all the battles of that long war, the echoes of which, audible but muted, reached that Burgundy farm.

We're sitting in the clearing of the Taboo and I'm fingering the grass growing out of the debris of that war which has just ended and is already obliterated.

"All night long," she says, "when the firing stopped, I waited for him to come, straining my ears listening to the sounds around the farm."

I'm crumpling the grasses, some of them are sharp-edged.

"I don't know why," she says, "but I kept thinking that he would appear, maybe at the back of the farm."

I chew on a stalk of grass, acid and fresh like the spring of the postwar, which is just beginning.

"I kept saying to myself that he was probably wounded," she says, "I heated some water and prepared some clean cloths to bind his wounds."

I recall that she was sixteen years old and I chew on the fresh, acid-tasting grass.

"Ma was crying in a room upstairs, she cried and cried and cried," she says.

I picture that night, the silence that had settled again over the Taboo heights, the trace of Hans, gone forever.

"At dawn I heard a rustling sound at the back door. It was only the wind," she says.

The winter wind over the burned-out heights of the Taboo.

"I kept on waiting, for days I waited, without hope," she says.

I lean back and bury my head in the tall grass.

"My mother went down to Dijon, that's where they had imprisoned the men," she says.

I look at the trees, at the sky between the trees, and try not to think about all that.

"I scoured the forest in every direction, I don't know why, but I had to do it," she says.

She had to discover some trace of Hans, but there was no longer any trace of Hans.

"Even now," she says, "I sometimes come here and wait."

I look at the sky between the trees, at the trees, I try to empty myself of all waiting.

"My brother hasn't come back either," she says.

I turn over on my side and look at her.

"Did you know he was German?" she says.

Surprised, I sit up on one elbow and look at her.

"He used to recite a song," she says, "something about the month of May."

Then I lie back down again, my head buried in the tall grass. I can feel my heart beating against the damp earth of the clearing, and again it's the month of May—im wunderschönen Monat Mai, als alle Knospen sprangen—the wonderful month of May / when all the buds are blooming. I feel my heart suddenly beating, I remember that march in the night that has been haunting my memory these past days. I can hear her stirring beside me, a rustling of grass, and her hand is caressing my close-cropped hair. It's not a caress, it's not even a friendly gesture, it's the touch of a blind person trying to find where he is, as if she were exploring the meaning of this close-cropped hair.

"You had your head shaved," she says.

I turn over toward her. She's stretched out beside me, her eyes wide open.

"Do you think my brother will still come back?" she asks.

So I whisper to her the story of that march in the night across Europe, which is one way of replying, the story of that long march that Piotr and his men took in the night of Europe. She listens avidly. And again it's the month of May in the clearing of the Taboo.

"You know how it is," says the voice behind me, "we split up into little groups and we never saw the guys who stayed behind to cover us."

The guy from Semur looks at the man talking and when he has finished he turns to me.

"He was a pal of yours, a good pal?" he asks.

"Yes," I say.

The guy from Semur shakes his head, and again there is silence in the half-light of the boxcar. This news of the end of the Taboo group is a low blow, a blow in the pit of my stomach, revealed by chance during this voyage. I won't know what happened to Hans until this voyage is over. And if I never return from this voyage, I'll never know what happened to Hans. If he remained behind in the covering group, I'll have to get used to the idea that Hans is dead. During the coming days, the coming weeks, these months advancing toward me, I'll have to get used to the idea that Hans is dead, that is, that idea (if one can call that opaque,

evanescent reality of the death of someone close to you an
"idea") will have to get used to me, will have to become
a part of my life. I have a feeling it will take time. But
maybe I won't have the time to get used to the idea of
Hans' death, maybe the advent of my own death will deliver
me from this concern. In the spongy mass that sits behind
my forehead, between my painful neck and burning temples,
where all the throbbing pains in my body, which is breaking into a thousand pieces of sharp glass, in that spongy
mass from which I would like to be able to draw with
both hands (or rather with delicate tongs, once the bony
plate which covers it has been lifted) the cotton-like fila-
ments, streaked perhaps with blood, which must fill all
the cavities and keep me from thinking clearly, which be-
cloud the whole interior, what they call consciousness, into
that spongy mass there works its way the idea that perhaps
my death will not even manage to be something real, that
is, something that belongs to someone else's life, at least
one person's. Perhaps the idea of my death as something
real, perhaps even that possibility will be denied me, and I
cast about desperately to see who might miss me, whose life
I might affect, might haunt by my absence and, at that
precise moment, I find no one, my life hasn't any real
possibility, I wouldn't even be able to die, all I can do is
efface myself, quietly eliminate myself from this existence,
Hans would have to be alive, Michel would have to be
alive for me to have a real death, a death somehow linked
to reality, for me not to vanish completely into the stench-
filled darkness of this boxcar.

When Dr. Haas asked me for my identification papers
at Epizy, that is, in Irène's house near Joigny, and obviously
I didn't yet know it was Dr. Haas, I merely came out into
the kitchen still half-asleep and Irène said to me in a soft,
perfectly calm voice: "It's the Gestapo, Gérard," she was
smiling, I caught a vague glimpse of three silhouettes, two

men and the blond woman, the interpreter, I learned that
later, and one of the men barked: "Your papers!" or some
such thing, anyway something easy enough to understand,
and then I tried to pull out my Smith and Wesson, no, that
day I had a Canadian revolver, the cylinder didn't rotate
laterally, it had a break-open action, but I couldn't complete my move, the cylinder must have got caught in the
leather belt, it didn't come, and the second man knocked
me out by hitting me in the neck, I fell to my knees, all I
could think about was pulling out my gun, having the
strength to pull out my gun and fire at that character in the
soft felt hat, that man with the gold teeth from one side
of his mouth to the other, that was the only important thing
I had left to do, disengage the revolver and fire at this guy,
the only thing upon which I could concentrate my attention,
my life; but the man in the felt hat in turn hit me as hard
as he could with the butt of his pistol on the top of my
head, his mouth open in a fixed grin full of gold teeth, the
blood spurted out into my eyes, which were already hazy,
the blond woman began to scream and for the life of me
I couldn't get that fucking Canadian revolver out. My face
was full of blood, that insipid warmth was the taste of life,
I was thinking in some strange state of exaltation, not imagining that, for the moment at least, the man in the soft
hat could do anything else but fire at me point-blank, seeing the grip of my revolver which I was still vainly trying
to work free. And yet even at that moment I was unable
to think of that death, however close and credible, as a
necessary reality; even then, at the very minute when it
seemed to be descending upon me, when, logically, it should
have descended upon me, death remained beyond, outside,
like an unrealizable thing or event as, on the plane of in-
dividuality alone, it in fact is. Later, each time I came into
close contact with death (as if death were an accident, or
some solid obstacle which one stumbles against, strikes,

runs into) the only real sensation it aroused in me was an acceleration of all the vital faculties, as if death were something you could ponder with all the variations, forms and nuances of thought, but in no way something that could happen to you. And it actually is like that, dying is the only thing that can happen to me which I shall never experience personally. But Hans' death was indeed something that had happened to me, that would henceforth be part of my life.

Then, a blank. For sixteen years I've been trying to seize those few hours between the conversation with the guy from the Taboo underground and the maniacal night awaiting us, trying to pierce the haze of these few hours which obviously must have passed, to seize piece by piece the reality of these hours, but almost in vain. Sometimes, in a flash, I remember not what happened, for nothing ever did, at any time during this voyage, but the memories and dreams that plagued me or filled my mind during these missing hours, that are missing in the perfectly remembered recollection of this voyage, where nothing else is lacking, neither the landscape nor a word of what was said, not one second of these interminable nights; so full of memory, in fact, that if I were to devote myself to relating all the details and detours of this voyage, I might risk seeing the people around me who had consented to hear me, even if only to be polite, grow weary and bored and then die, sliding softly off their chairs, plunging into death as into the almost stagnant water of my story, or else I might see them slowly going mad, raving mad perhaps, refusing any longer to bear the complacent horror of all the details and detours, the comings and goings of this long voyage of sixteen years ago. Here, of course, I'm summarizing. But still, having come this far, it annoys me not to be able to seize completely, not to be able to provide a second-by-second account of these few hours which defy me and sink deeper and deeper each time I flush out some prey, however insignificant, from the lost memory of those hours.

All I find is an occasional scrap here and there. Thus, it must have been during these hours that there occurred—since a minute-by-minute reconstruction of the entire voyage failed completely to fit it in—that dream, or that memory which stood out clearly from the rest of the confusion, like some blindingly clear light in the surrounding fog, the dream or the memory of that calm place with the smell of wax (the books, rows and rows of books) where I sought refuge, to which I fled from the fetid dampness of the boxcar, that deep silence smelling of wax and oak, of waxed oakwood, into which I plunged to escape from the ever increasing commotion of the car which soon, at nightfall, reached its climax. I do not believe that I succeeded in identifying this place during the voyage itself, this quiet place, the kind of ideal place one dreams about, filled with the sound of rustling pages, pages being thumbed through, the smell of paper and ink mixed with the odor of wax, and that vague impression that this place was itself surrounded by calm, by a muted silence, bare trees, all that not really clear, not a certainty but a vague suspicion of that quiet place mounted in a setting of total calm. Later, of course, it was no problem to pinpoint this dream, or memory, this nostalgia which was both hazy and clear, brilliant and opaque, in the midst of this very real nightmare of the boxcar. It was Martinus Nijhoff's bookshop, or more precisely the second story of his bookshop in The Hague. Today, twenty-three years later, I could still climb that stairway with my eyes closed, I would still feel perfectly at home among the long rows of books on the second story. Nijhoff generally remained on the ground floor, and he used to watch me, with his eyes twinkling behind the gold-rimmed lenses of his glasses, as I walked through the shop on my way to the stairs. On the second story were to be found the shelves of French books, both used and new, and I would spend hours there reading books I couldn't afford to buy. The big room was bathed in a soft light, that beautiful, dense light, with no sharp edges, of Nordic winters, a spherical luminosity flooding equally both foreground and background, filtering into that big room crowded with stern bookshelves (and that odor of wax in a way becoming the tangible equivalent of the somewhat haughty, terribly fragile, actually ridiculous puritanism of the whole) through the stained-glass windows ribbed with lead around each of the colored pieces of glass set here and there in keeping with some outmoded, slightly monotonous pattern. But all that, of course, does not belong to this particular dream in the course of the voyage. That dream was merely the longing for that quiet, closed-in place, not clearly identified, not linked with anything except the uncertain feeling of an irreparable loss, in the damp stench of the boxcar, which was soon filled with wild, disordered cries. Neither the smiling, benign air of Nijhoff's shop, nor the avenues stripped bare by winter, nor the frozen canals, nor the long race after school—the Tweede Gymnasium—to this quiet, closed-in place, belong to this dream, or rather to this sharp but slightly blurred memory which assailed me during these dismal hours, between the conversation with the guy from the Taboo and the *Walpurgisnacht* which awaited us. This quiet, closed-in place was only one of the points around which was constructed my childhood universe, breached on all sides by the rumbling rumors of the world, the blaring of the radio during the Anchluss in Vienna and the dull, stupid stupor of September, 1938, when the defeat of my country was assured, battered from all sides, like the Scheveningen dikes, beyond the trees and the dunes against which the tides of the equinox rolled and broke, the sea you had to lift your eyes to see, or climb up to, beyond the trees and the dunes, the sea which seemed forever

on the verge of surging down upon the solid earth below.
These long sessions of reading at Martinus Nijhoff's shop
were only a pause, and this presentiment already disturbed
me, on the long road of exile which had begun in Bayonne,
no, which had actually begun before, that night when we
were rudely awakened, in that house at the foot of the
tract of pines where we spent our last vacation, the whole
village setting out walking, in the gasping silence, when
the sudden conflagration of the hills and the arrival of the
refugees from the nearest village, off to the East, announced
the approach of Gambara's Italian troops devastating the
Basque country. (At the approach to the bridge the men
had erected a barricade of sacks of salt, they had shotguns,
tin cans filled with dynamite, I knew some of them, fisher-
men I had met down at the port over a period of several
summers, pelota players who used to go up to Mendeja,
on the pediment next to the old church, to begin once
again, as they had eternally in the past, their eternal game
between rival teams, the leather ball smacking against their
bare hands or, with an excruciating noise, striking the iron
strip which marked the lower limit of the game's surface
on the opposite wall; they looked up at the hills aglow with
fire, they clutched their shotguns to their chests, they went
on smoking in silence; to leave them behind, to leave that
barricade, which was totally inadequate in the face of
Gambara's tanks, was to cut the most essential ties, to set
forth on the road to exile, and suddenly you wished you
could age several years overnight and remain with them,
you vaguely promised yourself, with some terrible childish
despair, to make up for this delay, make up for the lost
time, somehow; but we were already leaving, wandering
aimlessly away in the nocturnal wave of that crowd, clad
in their espadrilles, which make a harsh, slapping noise
as they follow the asphalt coastal road overlooking the sea
and the sound of the breakers; yes, we were departing, we

had left, and it would be years, a long night of years marked by fires and gunfire, before we would take our places, before we would be able to take our places beside other men, the same men, behind other barricades, the same barricades, the same unfinished combat.) In Nijhoff's shop, the smell of wax, the sound of pages rustling, the benumbing heat after the long race past the frozen canals, between the phantom trees laid bare by the winter, was only a relatively short pause in that interminable voyage of exile.

In any case, the guy from Semur didn't say a word during these few hours which preceded the *Walpurgisnacht*, the last night of this voyage. Maybe he was already dying, that is, maybe death was already beginning to assemble its forces and ruses for a final assault, a sudden attack through the arteries, a cold clot of darkness advancing. Anyway, he didn't say a word. In a little while he's going to open his mouth, in a burst of ultimate despair, "Don't leave me alone, pal," and he's going to die, that is, his death will be finished. In fact, all conversation ceased, all words were stilled, during these hours. We were in a collective daze, a viscous silence, boiling like so many bubbles of restrained cries, of sudden outbursts of anger or terror, in concentric circles, where now it was no longer you or he or I who was shouting or whispering but the sticky dough we had become, all hundred and nineteen anonymous mouths, until the final burst of despair, of nerves completely shattered, the last vestiges of self-control exhausted.

Now that I think of it, I also must have spent some time at Martinus Nijhoff's during the spring months, the time of fresh green trees and water moving sluggishly in the canals, but the memory that always spontaneously arises is the grating-white memory of winter, of bare trees standing out starkly against the gray but infinitely iridescent light, which finally makes you wonder whether it's real or the light of the painters you used to go to see in the Rijksmuseum or the Boymans Museum, the light of Delft or the light of Vermeer van Delft. (And it's easy to see that the question is oddly complicated by the fact that certain of Vermeer's paintings are forgeries, that is, forgeries so well done, which relate so perfectly to the light I'm referring to that it's ridiculous to try and determine who imitated whom, maybe it was Vermeer who, anticipating by several centuries, imitated van Meegeren, and anyway, what difference would it make, I ask you, in the villa at Cimiez where van Meegeren had lived during the German occupation, and where I spent several days visiting friends who were then living there, what a pity it was that there was not a single van Meegeren forgery or real Vermeer left, since it was the forgery of the paintings by the forger which carried to their ultimate perfection the truth to which Vermeer first gave shape, the truth of that gray light, iridescent from within, which enveloped me as I ran past the bare trees toward Martinus Nijhoff's bookshop.)

So I used to run, in desperation, toward this quiet, cozy place, but just as I got there, just as the memory seemed to be getting clear, or perhaps I was on the verge of recognizing, of pinpointing the place, a jolt of the panting bodies, a sharp cry risen from the very depths of terror, unremittingly, seized me again, pulled me back, returned me to the reality of the nightmare of this voyage.

"We must do something, men," says a voice behind us.

I can't see very well what there is to be done except to wait, keep a grip on oneself, resist. Nor does the guy from Semur see either, he shakes his head doubtfully, or maybe he's simply in a daze. But whenever the situation becomes untenable, there's always someone who emerges to take charge, there's always a voice rising out of the mass of anonymous voices, saying what has to be done, pointing out the paths, even though they may be hopeless, often are hopeless, and harness the latent, scattered energies. On these occasions, when that voice resounds as it always does, the simple, shapeless agglomeration of human beings assembled by chance reveals a hidden structure of available wills, an astonishing plasticity which takes shape according to certain lines of force, reveals plans and projects which are perhaps unfeasible but which lend a meaning, a coherence to even the most absurd, the most desperate of human acts. And that voice inevitably makes itself heard.

"Men, we have to do something," that voice behind us says.

It's a clear, precise voice which cuts across the hubbub of the other terrified voices, at their last gasp. Suddenly people are suffocating, suddenly they can't bear it any longer, suddenly the guys begin to faint, to collapse, dragging others with them as they fall, those who fall beneath the mass of bodies suffocating in turn, pushing with all their might to work free, but they can't, it's practically impossible, shouting all the louder, screaming that they're going to die, the racket is deafening, total chaos, you feel yourself being pushed and pulled from side to side, you stumble over the fallen bodies, you're drawn toward the center of the car, shoved back again toward the sides, and the guy from Semur has his mouth open like a fish, trying to swallow as much air as he can, "give me your hand," an old man calls out, "my leg is caught under there, it's going to break off," the old man shouts, and someone else, over on the right, is striking out around him like a madman, blindly, they grab his arms, he squirms free with a wild scream, finally they knock him out, he falls and is trampled on, "this is madness, men, get hold of yourselves, keep your heads," someone says hopelessly, "water, we need some water," someone else says, "that's easy enough to say but where in the hell do we find water," and then, at the other end of the car, that lament, that interminable, inhuman lament which you still hope will not stop, for if it does it

will mean that that man, that animal, that creature making
it is dead, that inhuman lament is the sign of someone still
struggling to live, the guy from Semur has a man beside
him who has just fainted, almost doubled over, he clutches
at me, I try to support myself by hanging onto the side of
the car toward which, little by little, we've all been pro-
jected, I straighten up as best I can, the guy from Semur
manages to regain his balance, he smiles but says nothing,
he doesn't say another word, a long time ago I remember
having read about a fire at the *Novedades*, a theater, there
was a panic, people trampled on, but maybe, and this is a
point I'm unclear about, maybe it was only something I
read in a newspaper I had filched, maybe it was the memory
of a story I had heard, maybe the fire at the *Novedades* and
that panic occurred before I was old enough to read about
it myself under the table in the living room, in a newspaper
I had filched, I'm not clear on this point, it's a question of
no importance, I wonder how I can be concerned about
such a question now anyway, what difference does it make
whether I heard it from the lips of some adult, maybe
from Saturnina, or whether I read about it myself in a
newspaper whose front page must have carried streaming
headlines about such a fascinating news item.

"Listen, men, you've got to give me a hand," says the
guy again.

"Give you a hand?" I ask.

He's obviously talking to me, to the guy from Semur too,
to everybody around us who hasn't been grabbed, knocked
down, shoved, put out of action by the storm of panic
breaking loose in the boxcar.

"We've got to revive the guys who have fainted and get
them back on their feet," says the man who has taken
charge of the situation.

"Not a bad idea," I say, still unconvinced.

"Otherwise they're going to be trampled, or they'll suffocate, some of them killed maybe," he says.

"I'm sure you're right," I tell him, "but we're going to have our share of dead in any event."

The guy from Semur is listening, he's shaking his head, his mouth is still wide open.

"You have to find me some receptacles," the guy says in an authoritative tone, "empty tin cans, anything."

Mechanically I glance about, my eyes searching for some empty tin cans, anything, like the guy says.

"What do you want them for?" I ask.

I can't for the life of me see what he wants with receptacles, with empty tin cans, anything, as he says.

But the authoritative voice begins to have its effect. From this side and that they call out to him, in the screaming, humid half-light of the car hands stretch out to him, offering a certain number of empty tin cans.

I watch the guy, watch what he's going to do, the way you watch someone at the circus getting ready for his act, and you're still uncertain whether he's going to use these plates and balls to juggle with, or whether he's going to make them disappear or turn them into live rabbits, white pigeons or into bearded ladies or sweet, absent-looking lovely young ladies clothed in pink tights sprinkled with shiny sequins. I watch him as I watch the circus, I still can't get interested in what he's doing, I'm simply curious as to whether or not he's going to bring it off.

The guy picks the largest tin cans and discards the others.

"All right, men," he says, "all of you who can have to piss in these cans, I want you to fill them up for me."

The guy from Semur's lower jaw drops in amazement, he shakes his head even faster. But I think I've guessed what this guy is driving at, I think I've understood his act.

"We haven't any water, men," he says, "so we're going to

soak some handkerchiefs in the urine, we'll put the dampened handkerchiefs outside in the night air, which will give us cold compresses to revive the ones who have fainted."

Which is more or less what I had guessed.

The guys around me start pissing in the tin cans. When they're full, the guy starts to pass them around, he collects the handkerchiefs which he dips into the urine and then hands to those nearest the openings so they can shake them out in the cold night air. Then, following this guy's orders, we set to work. We pick up those who have collapsed, we press the cold, damp handkerchiefs to their faces and foreheads, we move them as close as we can to the cold night air, which revives them. The fact of having something to do sustains the others, those who were still all right, it calms them and gives them renewed strength. Starting in our corner, calm moves progressively forward, in concentric circles, toward the rest of the car.

"While the handkerchiefs are on your faces," the guy says, "keep your mouths and eyes closed."

The panic slowly subsides. There are still some guys fainting, but they are immediately taken in hand and pushed over to the openings, to the men with the tin cans full of urine. They are brought around, sometimes with the help of a few solid slaps and the damp, cold handkerchiefs on their unconscious faces.

"My can's empty," someone says, "anyone around who can fill it for me?"

"Pass it over," says another, "I've got some for you."

Which even sparks some scattered laughter. Barracks humor.

There are some, of course, we can't bring around, for whom we can do nothing. They were just plain dead. Dead as doornails. We collected them next to the first corpse of the voyage, next to the little old man who said: "What do you know about that!" and died a moment later. We collected them so they wouldn't be stepped on, but it was no easy matter in the damp disorder of the car. The simplest way to do it was to keep the corpses in a horizontal position and pass them, still horizontal, from hand to hand, over to the spot where we had decided to put them. Borne by invisible arms, their staring eyes open on a world gone dark, the corpses looked as if they were advancing by themselves. Death was stalking through the boxcar, silently, an irresistible force seemed to be pushing these corpses toward their ultimate act. I was later to learn that, in similar fashion, our German fellow-prisoners used to bear the bodies of those inmates who had died in the course of the day out onto the square where roll call was held. This was in the early days, the heroic period, when the camps were real camps; now, it seems, they are mere rest camps by comparison, at least such was the contemptuous opinion of the older prisoners. The S.S. used to inspect the impeccable ranks of the inmates, lined up in squares, section by section. The dead were in the center of the square, standing, putting on a bold front, supported by invisible hands. In the glacial cold of Ettersberg, beneath the Ettersberg snow and the rain streaming down into their dead eyes, the bodies grew quickly stiff. The S.S. made their count and it was this count, verified not once but twice, which determined the next day's rations. With the bread of the dead, with the dead's ration of margarine, with their soup, the prisoners established a reserve of extra food to help the ill and infirm. On roll-call square, with the Ettersberg rain streaming into their lifeless eyes, the snow sticking to their eyelashes and hair, the bodies of the fellow-inmates who had died during the day rendered a proud service to the living. They helped, temporarily at least, to overcome the death which constantly stalked the living.

It was at that point that the train stopped once again.

Silence settled over the car, a very special kind of silence, not the silence produced by the momentary, random absence of surrounding noise, but a silence of watching and waiting, of people holding their breath. And once again, as it has every time the train has stopped, a voice wants to know whether we're there, men.

"Are we there, men?" the voice asks.

Once again, nobody replies. In the night, the train blows its whistle, twice. Tense, painfully attentive, we strain our ears to hear. The guys even forget to faint.

"What do you see?" someone asks.

Which is another customary question.

"Nothing," someone who is near an opening says.

"No station?" they ask.

"I told you, nothing," is the answer.

Suddenly the sound of boots on the roadbed.

"They're coming."

"It must be a patrol, they patrol every time we stop."

"Ask them where we are."

"Yes, someone ask them if we're almost there."

"You think they're going to answer you?"

"They don't give a goddamn whether we're fed up."

"Damn right, that's not what they're paid for."

"Once in a while you run into a decent one and they do reply."

"Balls!"

"Shut the hell up. It's happened to me."

"You're the exception that proves the rule, buddy."

"No kidding, once in Fresnes prison . . ."

"Don't tell us the story of your life, you're boring us stiff."

"I'm telling you, once it did happen to me, that's all."

"Come on, shut up and let us listen!"

"There's nothing to hear, they're making the rounds, that's all."

The sound of the boots approaches, now they're next to the boxcar.

"It's one soldier. He's all alone," someone near the opening whispers.

"Ask him, for Christ's sake, what have you got to lose?"

"Sir," the man says, "hey, sir!"

"Shit," someone says, "that's no way to talk to a kraut."

"What the hell," the other one says, "we're asking him for some information, we have to be polite."

Cynical laughter.

"That real French courtesy will be the end of us yet," says a sententious voice.

"Excuse me, sir, can you tell me whether we'll be there soon?"

Outside, the soldier answers, but we can't make out what he's saying, he's too far away.

"What's he saying?" someone asks.

"Wait a minute, dammit, he'll tell us later."

"Of course we are," the guy says, "we're at the end of our rope in here."

Outside, the German's voice can again be heard, but we still can't make out what he's saying.

"Is that true?" says the guy talking with the German soldier.

Again, this invisible soldier's voice mutters something, outside, indistinctly.

"Well, thank you, thanks very much, sir," the guy says.

The sound of the boots can be heard again on the road-bed, moving away.

"Jesus Christ, man, are you polite!" says the same man as a' while before.

"So what did he say?"

Questions are being fired from all sides.

"Let him tell us, for God's sake, instead of braying like asses," someone yells.

So the guy tells.

"Well, when I asked him whether we'd be there soon, he answers: 'Are you really in such a hurry to arrive?' And he shakes his head."

"He shook his head?" someone off to the right asks.

"That's right, he shook his head," says the guy who's relating his conversation with the German soldier.

"As if to say what?" asks the same guy off to the right.

"Jesus, what a bore! What the hell difference does it make whether he shakes his head?" someone else shouts.

"As if to say that if he were in our shoes he wouldn't be in such a hurry to arrive," says the one who spoke with the German soldier.

"And why not?" someone at the end of the car asks.

"Come on, shut up, are we almost there or aren't we?" an exasperated voice cries out.

"He said we were there, or practically there, that we're about to be switched onto the tracks leading to the camp station."

"We're going to a camp. What kind of camp?" asks a surprised voice.

A chorus of curses rises and envelops that voice full of surprise.

"Where did you think we were going, for Christ's sake, to a summer resort? Where the hell did you come from?"

The guy says nothing, he must be pondering that discovery.

"But why did he shake his head? I'd really like to know why he shook his head," says the same guy as a while back, insistently.

But nobody's paying any attention to him now. Everybody's reveling in the thought that the voyage will soon be over.

"You hear that, pal?" I say to the guy from Semur, "we're practically there."

The guy from Semur smiles faintly and shakes his head, the way the German soldier did a while ago, according to the fellow who talked to him. The idea that the voyage is practically over doesn't seem to overwhelm the guy from Semur.

"Anything wrong, pal?" I ask the guy from Semur.

He doesn't answer right away, and the train starts off with a sudden jerk and a loud squeal of the axles. It knocks the guy from Semur off balance, and I hold him up. His arms clutch at my shoulders, and the beam of a searchlight sweeping through the car lights up his face for a second. There's a fixed smile on his face, and a look of intense surprise. The pressure of his arms on my shoulders becomes convulsive, and in a low, rasping voice, he cries out: "Don't leave me, pal." I was going to tell him not to be silly, don't be silly, pal, how could I leave him, but suddenly his body stiffened and became heavy, I almost toppled over into the midst of that somber, gasping mass in the car, with, suddenly, this weight, this stonelike, dead weight on my neck. I try to support myself on my good leg, the one that isn't painful and swollen. I try to straighten up, at the same time to support this body which has become heavy, infinitely heavy, abandoned to its own dead weight, the weight of a whole life, suddenly vanished.

The train is moving along at a good clip, and I'm holding my pal from Semur under his arms. I'm holding him in my arms, the sweat is running down my face in spite of the cold night air streaming in through the opening, through which lights are now shining.

He said to me: "Don't leave me, pal," and I find that

ludicrous, since it is he who's leaving me, since he's the one
who has left. The guy from Semur won't know how this
voyage turns out. But maybe it's true, maybe I am the one
who left him, who abandoned him. In the half-light I try
to examine his face, now darkened, the expression of intense surprise he had when he asked me not to leave him.
But I can't do it, my pal from Semur is nothing but an un-
decipherable shadow, heavy to hold, in my clenched arms.
No one is paying us any heed, the living and dead welded
together, and with a great clatter of brakes we arrive, motionless voyagers, into an area of harsh lights and the
barking of dogs.

(Later, always, in the most secret, best protected recesses
of memory, that arrival at the camp station, among the
beech trees and tall pines, suddenly exploded, like a great
shower of flashing light and furious barking. In my memory,
every time it occurs, there is always a striking equivalent
between the sound and the light, the clamor, I'd be willing
to bet, of dozens of dogs barking and the blinding bright-
ness of all the lamps and searchlights, their icy light inundat-
ing the snow-covered landscape. Thinking back, the meticulous staging, the artful orchestration of every detail of that
arrival, the well-polished ritual-like mechanism, repeated a
thousand times, strikes one immediately. Actually it helps
you see things in a clearer perspective, its ridiculous sav-
agery makes you want to smile. Its doctored, Wagnerian
aspect. But after those four days, those five nights of gasping voyage, emerging suddenly from that interminable
tunnel, it is excusable. One couldn't help but be struck by
the exaggeration. Still today, in unexpected ways and at
the most ordinary moments, that spectacle explodes in my
mind. You're tossing the salad, voices are reverberating in
the courtyard, some tune too, perhaps, unbelievably coarse;
mechanically you toss the salad, you let your mind wander

in the heavy, insipid atmosphere of declining day, of courtyard noises, of all those interminable minutes which are a
whole other life, and suddenly, like a scalpel slicing cleanly
into the soft tender flesh, this memory explodes, greatly
exaggerated, terribly out of proportion. And if someone,
seeing you standing there petrified, asks: "What are you
thinking about?" you have to answer: "Nothing," of course.
It's first of all a memory difficult to communicate, and, besides, you have to work it out by yourself.)

"The end of the line. Everybody out," someone in the
middle of the boxcar shouted.

But no one is laughing. We're bathed in a brilliant light
and the noise of dozens of dogs barking furiously.

"What kind of circus is this?" says the guy who a short
while before had taken charge of the situation.

I turn toward the opening to try and see. The guy from
Semur is growing increasingly heavy.

Directly opposite us, five or six yards away from the boxcar, on a station platform illuminated by searchlights, a long
line of S.S. is waiting. They are as motionless as statues,
their faces concealed by the shadow of the helmets which
gleam beneath the electric lights. They stand with their legs
apart, their rifles propped against the boot of the right
leg, and gripped by the barrel at arm's length. Some have
no rifle, but a sub-machine gun suspended by a strap around
their chests. They are holding dogs on leashes, the police
dogs that are barking at us, at the train. Dogs that clearly
know the score. They know that their masters are going
to let them charge at these shadows scheduled to emerge
from the closed, silent cars. They bark furiously at their
future prey. But the S.S. are as motionless as statues. Time
passes. The dogs stop barking and lie down at the feet of
the S.S. growling, their backs bristling. Nothing moves,
nothing stirs in the S.S. lines. Behind them, in the sheet
of light from the searchlights, the tall trees tremble beneath

the snow. Silence falls again on this motionless scene, and I wonder how long it's going to go on. In the boxcar, no one moves, no one says a word.

Somewhere a curt order breaks the silence, and from all directions the noise of whistles rends the air. With one mechanical movement, the row of S.S. approaches the car. And the S.S. begin to howl as well. The noise is deafening. I see the S.S. grab the barrels of their rifles, the rifle butts swinging skyward. Then the sliding doors suddenly slam open, the light strikes us in the face and blinds us. Like some gutteral refrain, the cry which we already know, the cry the S.S. use to punctuate practically every order, resounds: "Los, los, los!" Jostling one another, in clusters of five or six, the guys begin to jump down onto the station platform. They sometimes misjudge their leap, or get in each other's way and land flat on their stomachs, sprawling spread-eagle in the muddy snow on the platform. At times they stumble beneath the hail of blows that the S.S., breathing heavily like lumberjacks hard at work, administer at random with the butts of their rifles. With open mouths, the dogs charge at the bodies. And above the mad commotion, resounding dryly above the swirling confusion, the eternal cry: "Los, los, los!"

There is a growing void around me, and still I'm holding the guy from Semur by his arms. I'm going to have to leave him. I'm going to have to jump down onto the station platform, into that mob of people, if I wait too long and jump down alone I'll have the blows all to myself. I already know that the S.S. don't like laggards. It's over, this voyage is over, I'm going to leave my pal from Semur. That is, it's he who has left me, I'm all alone. I lay down his body on the floor of the car, and it's as though I were laying down my own past, all the memories linking me to the world of the past. Everything I told him during these days and end-less nights, the story of the Hortieux brothers, life in the

Auxerre prison, and Michel and Hans, the guy from the Othe Forest, everything my life used to be is slated to disappear, since he is no longer here. The guy from Semur is dead and I'm alone. I think that he had said: "Don't leave me alone, pal," and I walk toward the door to jump onto the platform. I don't remember whether he had said that: "Don't leave me alone pal," or whether he had called me by my name, that is, by the name he knew me by.

Maybe he had said: "Don't leave me alone, Gérard," and Gérard jumps down onto the station platform, into the blinding light.

By chance he lands on his feet and manages to elbow his way out of the throng. Farther along, the S.S. are lining up the deportees in columns of five. He runs over and tries to slip into the middle of the column, but doesn't succeed. A surge of the crowd pushes him back toward the outside row. The column sets off at a brisk pace, and a blow from the butt of a rifle propels him ahead. The icy night air makes it hard for him to breathe. He lengthens his stride to put as much distance as possible between him and the S.S. trooper running beside him, on his left, panting like a bull. He glances at the S.S., whose face is twisted by a rictus. Maybe it's the effort, maybe the fact that he never stops screaming. Happily, he's not one of the S.S. with a dog. Suddenly, a sharp pain shoots through his right leg, and he realizes that he's barefoot. He must have hurt himself on some stone hidden in the muddy snow on the station platform. But he doesn't have time to worry about his feet. Instinctively, he tries to control his breathing, to adapt it to the rhythm of his stride. Suddenly he feels like laughing, he remembers the La Faisanderie stadium, the beautiful grass track among the spring trees. The thousand-meter race was three laps long. Pelletoux had made his bid on the turn of the second lap, and he had committed the error of meeting the challenge. It would have been better for him to let Pelletoux pass and to fall in right behind him. It would have been better for him to save his strength for the straight stretch to the finish line. True, it was his first thousand-meter race. Later he had learned how to pace himself.

"These guys are crazy."

He recognizes this voice on his right. It's the guy who

tried to restore some semblance of order in the boxcar a while ago. Gérard glances at him. The guy seems to recognize him too, he motions to him with his head. He looks behind Gérard.

"Your pal?" he says.

"In the boxcar," Gérard says.

The guy stumbles and catches himself adroitly. He seems in good shape.

"What do you mean?" he asks.

"Dead," Gérard says.

The guy glances at him.

"Jesus, I didn't see a thing," he says.

"Right at the end," Gérard says.

"His heart," the guy says.

A guy sprawls in front of them. They hurdle his body and keep going. Behind, things turn into a mess, and the S.S. intervenes, no doubt. They can hear the dogs.

"Have to keep close to the pack," the man says.

"I know," Gérard says.

Suddenly, he outdistances the S.S. who was running beside him, on his left.

"You weren't in a good spot," the man says.

"I know," Gérard says.

"Never on the outside," the man says.

"I know," Gérard says.

No mistake, these voyages are full of clear-headed characters.

They emerge onto a broad, brightly lighted avenue. The pace suddenly slows. In the beam of the searchlights, they march in step. On either side of the avenue tall columns rise, surmounted by eagles with folded wings.

"Jesus," the guy says.

A kind of silence falls. The S.S. must be catching their breath. The dogs too. You can hear the hiss of thousands of bare feet in the muddy snow covering the avenue. The trees are rustling in the night. Suddenly, it's very cold. Their feet are numb and stiff, like pieces of wood.

"Jesus!" the guy whispers a second time.

And you know what he means.

"These bastards think big," the guy says.

And he laughs derisively.

Gérard wonders what he means, exactly. But he doesn't feel like putting the question to him, why he says that the bastards think big. This abrupt slowing of the race, this stinging cold he suddenly becomes aware of, and the absence of his pal from Semur, overwhelm him. His swollen knee fills his legs, and his entire body, with painful throbs. But actually, it's obvious what he means. This avenue, these stone columns, these haughty eagles, are made to last. This camp toward which we're marching is no temporary establishment. Centuries ago, he already marched to one camp, in the Compiègne Forest. Maybe the guy on his right was also part of that march in the Compiègne Forest. These voyages are rife with coincidence. In fact, he would have to make an effort and figure out how many days away he was from that march in the Compiègne Forest, centuries away, it seemed to him. Say one day for the voyage from Auxerre to Dijon. There was the predawn awakening, the clamor throughout the prison, suddenly awakened, to shout good-bye to those leaving. From the gallery on the top story, Irène's voice had reached his ears. The guy from the Othe Forest had hugged him in his arms, on the threshold of cell 44.

"So long, Gérard," he had said, "maybe we'll meet again."

"Germany's a big place," he had answered.

"Still, maybe we will," the guy from the Othe Forest had insisted.

After that, the local railway to Laroche-Migennes. They

had had to wait a long time for the train from Dijon, at first in a café transformed into a Soldatenheim. Gérard had asked to go to the toilet. But the S.D. man in charge of the convoy hadn't removed the handcuff chaining him to the old peasant from Appoigny. He had had to drag the old man with him to go and piss, and besides he didn't have to piss. Under these conditions, he couldn't try a thing. Then they had waited out on the station platform, surrounded by sub-machine guns leveled at them. They're marching in step along that brilliantly lighted avenue, in the snow of early winter, and after this winter just beginning there will still be another long winter to come. He looks at the succession of eagles and emblems on the tall granite columns. The guy on his right looks too.

"You learn something new every day," he says with a knowing air.

Again Gérard tries to count the days of this voyage now ending, the nights of this voyage. But it's all terribly confused. They spent only one night in Dijon, that much is certain. After that, everything is more or less hazy. Between Dijon and Compiègne there was at least one stopover. He remembers one night in a barracks, a military compound, some dilapidated, decrepit administrative building. There was a stove in the middle of the hut, but no mattresses, no blankets. In one corner, some men were quietly singing, "You won't have Alsace or Lorraine," and he found it ridiculous and touching. Some others, crowded around a young priest, the tiresome kind who's forever trying to cheer you up, were cooking up some other magic. In Dijon, Gérard had already been obliged to make things very clear, to tell him, gently but firmly, that he had no need whatsoever of any spiritual comfort. A somewhat confused discussion about the soul followed, of which he retains a beguiling memory. He had rolled himself up into a ball in an isolated corner, his overcoat wrapped snugly about his legs, looking for a little peace, the evanescent happiness of being at peace with oneself, that serenity which comes from being master of your own life, in charge of yourself. But a young guy came over and sat down beside him.

"Got a smoke, pal?" he asked.

Gérard shakes his head no.

"I'm afraid I'm just not provident by nature," he adds.

The guy gives a high-pitched laugh.

"Jesus, me neither. I didn't even have the foresight to have myself arrested in winter clothes."

And again he laughs.

In fact, all he's wearing is a light jacket and trousers, and a shirt open at the collar.

"They brought me the overcoat while I was in prison," Gérard says.

"Because you have a family," the guy says.

Again, he gives this high-pitched laugh.

"Hell, such things do happen," Gérard says.

"You don't have to tell me," he says enigmatically.

Gérard glances at him. The boy looks a little drawn, a little frantic.

"If you don't mind," Gérard says, "I'm trying to get some rest."

"I need to talk," the other one says.

Suddenly, in spite of his thin, scarred face, he looks like a kid.

"Need?" Gérard asks, turning over toward him.

"For weeks I haven't had a chance to talk," the boy says.

"What do you mean?"

"I spent three months in solitary, that's all," the guy says.

"Sometimes, with Ramaillet, I said to myself that I would have preferred solitary," Gérard tells him.

"I would have preferred Ramaillet."

"It's as bad as all that?" Gérard asks him.

"I don't know your Ramaillet, but I can assure you I would have preferred Ramaillet."

"Maybe you don't know how to remain inside yourself," Gérard says.

"Inside?"

His nervous eyes are darting constantly back and forth.

"You settle yourself into immobility, you relax, you recite poetry, you recapitulate the errors you may have committed, you tell yourself the story of your life, tidying up an occasional detail, you try to recall the Greek conjugations."

"I never took Greek," the boy says.

They look at each other and both burst out laughing.

"That's a hell of a note, nothing to smoke," the boy says.

"Why don't you ask the gung-ho priest," Gérard says, "he might have something."

The other shrugs his shoulders sullenly.

"I keep asking myself what I'm doing here," he says.

"It's high time you found out," Gérard tells him.

"I'm working at it," the boy says. And he keeps on pounding his right fist into the hollow of his left hand.

"Maybe you should have stayed at home," Gérard says.

The other laughs again.

"It was my father who denounced me to the Gestapo," he says.

It was his father who denounced him to the Gestapo, merely to have peace and quiet at home, he said, and the Gestapo tortured him, his right leg bears the scars of the red-hot iron. He pulled up his trousers to his knee, but the scars go even higher, apparently, to the hip. He held out, he didn't denounce Jackie, the head of his underground network, and two months later, quite by chance, he learned that Jackie was a counter-spy. So he can't quite figure out what he's doing here, he's wondering whether he won't be compelled to kill his father, later on. (This story of Jackie reminds Gérard of the warning Irène had managed to send him in Auxerre. According to Irène, Alain had informed her that, to avoid further torture, London had authorized her to place herself at the disposal of German intelligence, while still continuing to work for Buckmaster in her new role. "Can you see me as counter-spy?" Irène asked, underlining the term "counter-spy" with a furious stroke of her pencil. Alain was a bastard anyway, you could tell by looking at him.) Marching in step down this monumental avenue toward the camp, Gérard wonders whether he'll run into this boy again there. He must be in the convoy, Gérard thinks he caught a glimpse of him the morning of their departure from Compiègne, as the S.S. were lining them up in a long column. In the darkened houses, the people were still curled up snug in their beds, or just getting ready for a new day of work. From time to time they heard an alarm clock going off in the darkened houses. The last noise of the old life was this sharp, abrupt sound of the alarm clocks setting in motion the mechanism of a new day of work. Here and there, a woman would crack open a window and look out into the street, no doubt attracted by this muffled noise, this rumbling of the interminable column marching to the station. The S.S. slammed closed the shutters of the ground floor windows. They hurled invectives at the higher windows, which they couldn't reach, and pointed their guns up at them. The heads quickly disappeared. They had already experienced that feeling of divorce, of being isolated in another universe, upon their arrival at Compiègne. They had made them get out at Rethondes, it was sunny that day. They had walked among the winter trees, and the sun gave the underbrush an iridescent look. After those long months of sweating stone and the hard-earth courtyard, without a blade of grass, without a leaf trembling in the wind or a branch snapping underfoot, it was pure joy. Gérard breathed in the odors of the forest. They felt like telling the German soldiers to knock this shit off, to let them loose so they could all wander away down the forest trails. Once, coming around the edge of a copse, he even saw an animal bound away, and his heart skipped a beat, as the saying goes. That is, his heart began to pound wildly, to follow the leaps of that doe, light and sovereign, from copse to copse. But there was also an end to that Compiègne Forest. He would gladly have walked for hours in that forest, despite the handcuff chaining him to Raoul, for in Dijon he had managed to have himself hand-cuffed to Raoul, before setting off on this long, uncertain journey. At least you could talk to Raoul. It was like pulling teeth to get anything out of the old man from Appoigny. There was also an end to that Compiègne Forest, and once again they were pounding the pavement of the Compiègne streets. As their column penetrated deeper into the city, six abreast, handcuffed two by two, a heavy silence fell. All you could hear was the sound of their footsteps, of their death marching. The people stood stock still on the side-walks, petrified. Some turned away their heads, others dis-appeared down the side streets. Remembering, Gérard thought that this blank look directed at them was the look of people contemplating the flood of beaten armies, falling back in disorder. He was marching in the outside right row of the column, at the edge of the pavement, and he tried to catch someone's eyes, but always in vain. The men bowed their heads or turned away. The women, sometimes holding children by the hand, he seemed to remember that it was about the time school gets out, did not turn their heads away, but their expressions were like fleeting water, an opaque dilated transparency. It took some time to cross the town, Gérard concentrated on trying to verify, sta-tistically, that initial impression. Yes, he was quite right, most of the men were turning away their heads, most of the women were looking at them with a totally blank expression.

He remembers two exceptions, though.

Hearing them pass, the man must have left his shop, perhaps a garage or some other mechanical enterprise, because he arrived wiping his black, greasy hands on a rag that was equally black and greasy. He was wearing a heavy turtle-neck sweater beneath his blue overalls. He came out onto the sidewalk wiping his hands, and when he saw what it was he didn't turn away his head. On the contrary, he let his attentive gaze absorb every detail of that scene. He certainly must have made a rough calculation as to how many prisoners that column contained. He must have tried to guess what parts of his country they came from and whether they were from the city or the country. He must have estimated the proportion of young in the column. His attentive gaze evaluated every detail, as he stood there on the edge of the sidewalk, drying his hands, with that slow, endlessly repeated gesture. As if he needed to keep on repeating this gesture, to keep his hands occupied, in order to reflect more freely upon every aspect of that scene. As if he first of all wanted to engrave it in his memory, so as to analyze later all the information that might be drawn from it. Every passing prisoner, in fact, by the way he looked, by his age and the way he was dressed, bore him a message concerning what was really happening in his country, an indication of the battles in progress, however distant. Of course, by the time Gérard thought all that, by the time he told himself that this man's attitude, his avidly attentive air, might mean all that, the man was left far behind, he had disappeared forever. But Gérard went on observing their marching column through the tense, burning, attentive look of that man now far behind, gone, certainly back at his work now on some precise, shiny machine, thinking about what he had just seen, while, mechanically, his hands were busy running the shiny, meticulous machine. Through the look that this unknown man had loaned him, Gérard noticed that the great majority of their marching column was composed of young men, and that these young men, you could tell from their heavy shoes, their leather jackets or fur-lined coats, their trousers torn by the brambles, were members of the maquis. They were not the anonymous gray-visaged individuals rounded up by chance in some city, but fighters. That is, their column gave an impression of strength, it clearly revealed a dense, complex truth of destinies engaged in a freely accepted, though uneven, combat. For this reason, the look that should have been directed at them was not that vague, fleeting light of frightened eyes, but a quiet look, like that man's look, a look of equals. And suddenly it seemed to Gérard that that man's look made their march not one of an army in rout, but rather a victorious march. And it didn't matter to him to think, to assume, that most of them were marching, with that victorious gait, toward a destiny that could not be anything but death. Their death-to-come marching purposefully through the streets of Compiègne, like a living wave. And the wave had grown, now it was parading down that Wagnerian-opera avenue, past these tall columns, beneath the dead look of Hitlerian eagles. The man in Compiègne, on the edge of the sidewalk, endlessly wiping his greasy hands, had smiled at Gérard when he came abreast of him, when he had passed him at a distance of no more than three feet. For a few brief seconds their eyes had met, and they had smiled at each other.

"What's going on?" the fellow on Gérard's right says.

The column has stopped.

Gérard cranes to look over the shoulders of those in front of him. In the distant dark, the two parallel rows of streetlights illuminating the avenue seem to converge on a dark mass, barring their way.

"That must be the entrance to the camp," Gérard says.

The man also looks and shakes his head.

"I wonder," he says, but he stops and doesn't say what it is he wonders.

On both sides of the avenue, in the luminous halo of the streetlights, loom the silhouettes of buildings of varying heights, set here and there among the trees of the forest.

"This damn place is as big as a city, Gérard says.

But the S.S. guard is back beside him and must have heard him talking.

"Ruhe!" he screams.

And he slams the butt of his rifle into Gérard's ribs.

At Compiègne, the woman had also just missed being hit in the face with a rifle butt. She hadn't turned her head away either. She hadn't allowed her gaze to grow glazed, like stagnant water. She had started to walk beside them, on the sidewalk, keeping in step with them, as though she herself wanted to assume a share, as large a share as possible, of the weight of their march. She walked with a proud step, in spite of her wooden-soled shoes. At one point she shouted something to them, but Gérard couldn't hear what it was. Something short, maybe only a single word, those who were marching at her level turned to her and made a sign to her with their heads. But this shout, this cry of encouragement, this word, whatever it was, to end the silence, or break the solitude, her own and that of the men, chained together by twos, crowded in against one another but still alone, since they were unable to express what they had in common, this shout attracted the attention of a German soldier who was walking a few steps ahead of her on the sidewalk. He turned and saw the woman. The woman was walking toward him, her step did not falter, and she surely didn't turn away her head. Head high, she bore down on the German soldier, and the German soldier screamed something at her, an order or an oath, a threat, his face a twisted mask of panic. At first, that expression of fear surprised Gérard, but it was not difficult to explain. Anything not in keeping with the over-simplified views of things which the German soldiers have, any unexpected gesture of revolt or firmness, must, indeed, frighten them to death. For it instantly suggests the full extent of a hostile universe surrounding them, even if the surface appears relatively calm, even if, on the surface, the relations between the occupation troops and the world around them are seemingly smooth. Suddenly, that woman bearing down upon him, her head high, marching along beside that column of prisoners, evokes a thousand realities for the German soldier, of shots in the night, of murderous ambushes, of partisans emerging out of the darkness. The German soldier screams with terror, despite the gentle winter sun, despite his comrades in arms marching before and behind him, despite his obvious superiority over this defenseless woman, over these men in chains, he screams and shoves his rifle butt into the woman's face. For several seconds they remain there face to face, he still screaming, and then the German soldier decamps to return to his place beside the column, not without casting one last hate-filled, fearful glance at the motionless woman.

Three days later, when they again marched through Compiègne on their way to the station, there was no one in the streets. There were only those faces, fleetingly glimpsed at a window now and then, and that piercing sound of alarm clocks in the still darkened houses.

Since the S.S. trooper had rejoined them, the man on his right had not uttered another word. They still are not moving. Gérard can feel the cold beginning to paralyze him, spreading, like a flow of icy lava, throughout his body. He makes an effort to keep his eyes open, to etch clearly in his memory the image of that long avenue flanked by tall columns, the dark mass of the trees and the buildings beyond the lighted area. He says to himself that an adventure such as this doesn't often happen, that he ought to take full advantage of it, fill his eyes with these sights. He looks at the tall columns, at the eagles of the thousand-year Reich, with their folded wings, their beaks raised high in the snowy night, in the light, diffused at that height and that distance, but extremely harsh and precise in the middle of the avenue where there are dozens of streetlights. The only thing lacking, Gérard tells himself, fighting to keep his eyes open, to keep from giving in now, right at the end of the voyage, to the benumbing torpor of the cold which is spreading throughout his body, spreading to his brain, which is beginning to set, as one says that a jelly, or mayonnaise or a sauce of any sort sets, the only thing lacking is some majestic, grandiose opera music which would carry the barbarous mockery to its ultimate limits, and it's strange that the S.S., at least some of them, the most imaginative, and God knows that the most imaginative S.S. have plenty of imagination, it's strange they haven't thought of this detail, of this final bit of stage-craft. But his eyes close, he stumbles forward, the incipient fall of his body rouses him from his torpor, he catches himself, regains his balance. He turns to the man on his right, and the man on his right saw it all, he edges imperceptibly closer to Gérard so that Gérard can lean on his left shoulder, his left leg. It's all right, pal, Gérard tells him in look and thought, since the S.S. trooper is still there keeping a close eye on them, it's all right, thanks, a rough moment to get through, we're almost there, thanks, pal, Gérard tells him without opening his mouth, without moving his lips, without uttering a word, just a look, the last thing left to us, this last human luxury, a free look, which the S.S. have no way of controlling. It's a limited language, true, and Gérard would have liked to tell his pal, whose left shoulder and left leg are helping to support him, but it's

impossible with the eyes alone to tell him of this idea that
occurred to him, about the music, a beautiful, noble, solemn
music floating over this snowy landscape and this inordi-
nate pride of stone eagles among the rustling trees of
January. If conversation had been possible, if the S.S.
trooper were not there beside them, watching, perhaps
with a smile, a lapse, his pal, who knows, might have been
able to explain to Gérard that there was no lack of music
in the S.S. ritual. On Sundays, for example, after the noon
roll call, throughout those interminable afternoons, the
loudspeakers broadcast music to every room, sometimes
waltz music and sometimes, though less often, concerts of
classical music. Perhaps, if it had been possible for that
conversation to take place, his pal, standing there in the
snow, waiting for the gates of that prison, toward which
they have been traveling for so many days, to open, might
have explained to him that they are going to spend certain
Sunday afternoons, when it rains, for example, or when it
snows, huddled around the table in the room, listening to a
Bach concerto, in the midst of all the commotion of those
idle afternoons, the hardest to bear, which lie ahead of
them. They might have come to the conclusion, if it had been
possible to hold that conversation, that only technical con-
siderations prevented the S.S. from using some carefully
chosen, noble, solemn musical score, to bring one final,
truly maniacal touch to their staging of the arrival before
the prison gates, perhaps nothing more than budgetary con-
siderations. On the other hand, there was music every
day of the year when the Kommandos left for work at dawn
and when they came back in the evening. But after giving
it a little more thought, it seems unlikely that they could
have come to that conclusion, even if it had been possible
to hold that conversation, it seems highly unlikely that his
pal would have been well enough informed about the
routine of that place toward which they were marching,

before whose gates they were standing motionless in the cold of that winter just beginning, and after this winter just beginning there will still be another long winter to come. It is certainly unlikely that this pal on whose left shoulder Gérard has found a support can tell him about this daily departure to music, on their way to work at the Gustloff factories, the Deutsche Ausrüstungs Werke, D.A.W. for short, the Mibau, this whole rosary of war factories surrounding the camp, within this second confine where, though they don't know it, they already are, the work in the quarries, the work of excavation. It is unlikely that, in the course of this conversation, assuming it could have taken place, they would have been sufficiently imaginative to guess that the members of this orchestra wore a uniform with red trousers tucked into their black boots and a green jacket with wide yellow sleeves and that they play stirring marches, something akin to circus music just before the elephants come on, for example, or before the arrival of the baby-faced equestrian sheathed in pink satin. Obviously, neither Gérard nor his pal could have been sufficiently imaginative, the reality of the camp orchestra, of these musical departures, of these weary returns to the sound of stirring, brassy, bombastic marches, this reality is still, though not for long, beyond the scope of their imaginations. Soon, after they have covered the few hundred years still separating them from the monumental gate of that enclosure, it will be meaningless to say that something, anything, is unimaginable, but for the moment they are still imbued with the prejudices, the realities of the past, which makes it impossible to imagine things which, in the final analysis, will be proved to be perfectly real. And as that conversation cannot take place, since the S.S. guard is there just waiting for the slightest infraction of the rules, the slightest slip, which will entitle him to finish off the fallen prisoner with a bullet in the back of the neck, and being no

longer able to follow the column, since silence and the practically clandestine support on the left shoulder of this guy
are the only recourse we have left, Gérard fights against the
sudden weakness of his own body, trying to keep his eyes
open, to let them absorb this icy light on the snowy landscape, these streetlights stretching down the monumental
avenue, flanked by tall columns of stone surmounted by the
hieratic violence of Hitlerian eagles, this mad landscape in
which only the noble, solemn music of some fabulous opera
is lacking. Gérard tries to engrave all this in his memory,
meanwhile vaguely thinking that it is well within the realm
of possibility that the impending death of all the spectators
may efface forever the memory of this spectacle, thinking what a shame that would be, he doesn't know why, his
brain was a heavy, cottony mass, but it would be a shame,
the certainty of this idea takes hold of him and suddenly it
seems to him that this noble, solemn music does strike up,
full and serene, in the January night, it seems to him that,
with this, they come to the end of the voyage, that this is
indeed the way, amid the echoing waves of that noble
music, in the icy light exploding into moving sprays, one
has to leave the world of the living, that ready-made phrase
whirls dizzily in the deep recesses of his brain, blurred like
a window by the raging gusts of rain, leave the world of
the living, leave the world of the living.

THE CASE OF SERGEANT GRISCHA by Arnold Zweig   1-58567-335-8

"The greatest novel on a war theme . . . from any country."   —J.B. PRIESTLEY

"Some experiences in literature are unforgettable and this is one novel that culminates in an overwhelming effect of power and protest and irony and pathos of human fate."   —*The New York Times*

THE SORROW OF BELGIUM by Hugo Claus   1-58567-238-6

"With biting wit, gorgeous language and graphic imagery, Hugo Claus rushes the reader back in time as if by magic . . . This immense autobiographical novel is clearly Claus' masterwork."   —DANIELLE ROTER, *The Los Angeles Times*

PAST CONTINUOUS by Yaakov Shabtai   1-58567-339-0

"I cannot recall having encountered a new work of fiction that has engaged me as sharply as *Past Continuous*, both for its brilliant, formal inventiveness and for its relentless, truth-seeking scrutiny of moral life."   —IRVING HOWE, *The New York Review of Books*

MOUNT ANALOGUE by René Daumal   1-58567-342-0

"A marvelous tale . . . as transparent and as inexhaustible as *Pilgrim's Progress* or a New Testament parable."   —ROGER SHATTUCK

"One of the most intriguing poetic reveries of contemporary literature."
                                              —ROBERT MALLET, *Le Figaro Littéraire*

A NIGHT OF SERIOUS DRINKING by René Daumal   1-58567-399-4

"The book is Daumal at his witty, satirical, parabolic best. It demolishes all ordinary human concepts and then, in a final redemptive gesture, sends its protagonists out into the resulting chaos to 'pursue the business of living.'"   —P.L. TRAVERS

GREEN HENRY by Gottfried Keller   1-58567-427-3

"In no literary works of the nineteenth century do the lines of development that to this day determine our lives become so clear to us as in those of Gottfried Keller. . . . His prose is unconditionally loyal to every living thing."   —W.G. SEBALD

THE OVERLOOK PRESS
WOODSTOCK & NEW YORK
www.overlookpress.com

THE MAN WHO CRIED I AM by John A. Williams   1-58567-580-8

"A blockbuster . . . an intensely American book—bitter, frank, honest. . . . At the same time, the book soars past American boundaries. Readers white and black may find in it either hope or terror."   —*The New York Times Book Review*

CASTLE GRIPSHOLM by Kurt Tucholsky   1-58567-558-X

"The first writers that come to mind when reading Tucholsky are Nabokov and Ford . . . a master of the studied nonchalance of the tidily perverse." —*The Times* (London)

HENRY, KING OF FRANCE by Heinrich Mann   1-58567-488-5

"The story moves swiftly, from scene to scene, almost like a play . . . The philosophy of the author, a philosophy touched by humor, shines transiently through the texture of the closely woven style."   —*Saturday Review*

YOUNG HENRY OF NAVARRE by Heinrich Mann   1-58567-487-7

"So sharply and tensely alive, so dramatic, so profound and beautiful, as to touch every chord of interest and significance and appreciation in the reader's mind."
—*The New York Times*

"Young Henry of Navarre is an important and, in some respects, a frightening historical novel. It is important in itself as a vital and colorful work."   —*The Nation*

Check our website for new titles

THE OVERLOOK PRESS
WOODSTOCK & NEW YORK
www.overlookpress.com